Praying *for* My Life

Also by
Marion Bond West

Out of My Bondage

No Turning Back

Two of Everything But Me

Look Out Fear, Here Comes Faith!

The Nevertheless Principle

PRAYING *for* MY LIFE

MARION BOND WEST

GuidepostsBooks™
New York, New York

Praying for My Life

ISBN 0-8249- 4705-3

Published by GuidepostsBooks
16 East 34ᵗʰ Street
New York, New York 10016
www.guidepostsbooks.com

Distributed by Ideals Publications, a Guideposts company
535 Metroplex Drive, Suite 250
Nashville, Tennessee 37211

GuidepostsBooks and *Ideals* are registered trademarks of Guideposts, Carmel, New York.

ACKNOWLEDGMENTS

All Scripture quotations, unless otherwise noted, are taken from the *New American Standard Bible*, © The Lockman Foundation, 1960, 1962, 1963, 1968, 1971, 1972, 1973, 1975, 1977. Used by permission.

Scripture quotations on pages 58, 218, 219 and 239 are taken from *The King James Version of the Bible*.

Scripture quotation on page 34 is taken from *The Holy Bible, New International Version*. Copyright © 1973, 1978, 1984 International Bible Society. Used by permission of Zondervan Bible Publishers.

Portions of chapter 21 are from "Looking Out My Kitchen Window" by Marion Bond West. Reprinted by permission of Abbey Press, St. Meinrad, Indiana.

A portion of chapter 41 appeared as "Smiling over Spilled Milk." From *HomeLife*, 1975. Copyright © 1975 by LifeWay Christian Resources of the Southern Baptist Convention. All rights reserved. Used by permission.

Library of Congress Cataloging-in-Publication Data

West, Marion B.
Praying for my life / Marion Bond West.
    p. cm.
ISBN 0-8249-4705-3
1. West, Marion B. 2. Christian biography. 3. Consolation. I. Title.
BR1725.W418A3 2006
277.3'083092—dc22

2006005714

Jacket photograph by Ray Massey/Getty Images
Designed by Marisa Jackson

Printed and bound in the United States of America

10 9 8 7 6 5 4 3 2 1

For all those who have almost given up hope

almost stopped believing

almost ceased praying . . .

a l m o s t .

CONTENTS |

PRAYING *for* MY LIFE

INTRODUCTION |

Though the fig tree should not blossom
And there be no fruit on the vines,
Though the yield of the olive should fail
And the fields produce no food,
Though the flock should be cut off from the fold
And there be no cattle in the stalls,
Yet I will exult in the Lord,
I will rejoice in the God of my salvation.
The Lord God is my strength,
And He has made my feet like hinds' feet,
And makes me walk on my high places.
                          —HABAKKUK 3:17–19

FOR THIRTY YEARS, I have loved and identified with this Scripture. It's from a tiny book—only three chapters. Pastors rarely preach from it. For years I didn't even know how to pronounce its name. But I loved to read the passage aloud, marveling at the rhythm and beauty of the words and at the prophet's astonishing faith—his stubborn, determined faith that nothing could alter.

Nothing.

As my own faith began to be tested some time ago, I'd find myself praying like Habakkuk, just to see what it felt like. Sometimes I wasn't certain I really meant it, but the more I prayed my situation into Habakkuk's declaration of faith, the more I did, truly, mean it.

Though my husband does not get healed, and the new CAT scan doesn't show what we want, and I have to raise these children alone, and I have no idea how to do that, I will put my total trust in the Lord. He'll have to show me how to get through this. He'll have to show me step by step.

Ever since I was a small child I've been afraid of getting lost. One day, driving on an unfamiliar expressway heading toward South Carolina (I live in Georgia, and I hadn't wanted to go to South Carolina), I prayed out loud:

"Though I've taken the wrong exit and have no idea where I am and don't know how to turn around and am about to burst out crying and it feels as though I may just drive off the face of the earth and I'm becoming more frightened by the mile, I will, yes indeed, I will trust in God—the God who saved me and who knows exactly where I am. I'm going to praise Him right now and believe that He'll show me a way to turn around. He can do it!"

Through the years I've mentioned these verses of Habakkuk to friends, and even to strangers. Once in a while someone else will get excited about it with me. But a lot of people just let me go on and on and then excuse themselves from the conversation.

Then in April of 2001 I was having lunch with Karen Barber, a writer friend of mine. We'd spent some time in prayer before eating, and so as we ate our salads I mentioned Habakkuk 3:17–19. "I can't believe no one's written a book about this Scripture, Karen. It's so powerful and. . . ."

"Did you ever think that you are that someone, Marion?" Karen asked.

"No, no, not me! No more books and no more children."

She smiled. "Have you prayed about it?"

I shook my head, my salad forgotten. "I don't want to do another book. I'm *not* going to do one!"

Karen graciously dropped the subject, but a few days later I got a note from her. She assured me that she was continuing to pray about two important matters in my life and added, "I'm also praying about the book of encouragement that you aren't writing."

My mouth flew open. Just two days before in church, for some crazy reason I'd made a hurried outline of a book. The section titles were verses from Habakkuk 3. *Just to enjoy writing the words,* I told myself.

Still clutching Karen's note, I phoned her. My mouth was suddenly dry and my heart was pounding. She answered on the second ring. "Karen," I said, "I made an outline in church Sunday, but I couldn't possibly write a book! I'm just playing around with the words—sort of like a crossword puzzle. Anyway, I've never written a book or an article from an outline. I don't even know how to make an outline!"

She laughed—a kind of holy laughter—and added gently, "Oh, I think God's had you in mind for a book like this for a long time now."

Though I have no idea how to write another book—even about Habakkuk 3:17–19, and I don't have the time or energy and probably no one would want to publish it, and I'd just be working hard for nothing, and most likely no one would want to read such a book . . .

Yet, I will trust You, Lord. You'll have to show me exactly how to do this, step by step, and give me tons of strength and enthusiasm, because right now it seems like a ridiculous idea. Totally impossible.

PART ONE

"THOUGH THE FIG TREE SHOULD NOT BLOSSOM..."

1 | THE CHOICE

THE OVERWHELMING TEMPTATION to panic was as real as the green kitchen telephone I held in my hand. The desire to throw down the phone, jump in the car and drive somewhere—anywhere altogether carefree—pulled at me like an undertow.

You've been here before, I tried to reason with myself. *You've been sent back to the fear again, just by the phone ringing.* If this had been my first experience with fear, I would have immediately surrendered, never suspecting that I had a choice. How many times had I thought: *Who can stand against this? No one! It would be like standing in front of a steamroller or a freight train.*

I swallowed twice, took a deep breath, and tried to speak in a normal voice. "Yes, this is Marion, Jeremy's mother."

This can't be anything but bad news. You don't get good news from hospital chaplains.

"You need to come to the emergency room now. Jeremy is in stable condition, but you need to get here. He's been in a serious accident."

I wanted to ask for details. Is he conscious? Is anyone else hurt? Silently I told myself, *Don't do that. It will invite the panic to swarm all over you.*

"We're leaving now," I replied, surprised at the normalcy of my voice.

"Gene!" I shouted to my husband, who was watching the

news on television. "Jeremy's been in another wreck. He's in the hospital this time. Let's go!"

Our eyes met, and we stared at each other without speaking. We'd run out of words. This was Jeremy's fourth auto accident in a matter of weeks. He'd been diagnosed as bipolar six months ago. Since then he'd been in a behavioral facility four times, but once out, he didn't take his medicine. Depression now had a fierce grip on him.

Gene nodded, and we headed for the car. We'd been married sixteen years—we married four years after Jeremy's father died. Jeremy and his brother Jon—fraternal twins—had just turned fifteen when they lost their father. In some ways, they still seemed fifteen, though they were now thirty-five. Neither had married.

At the hospital, we made our way past the trauma patients in the crowded ER. Finally we reached the room where Jeremy lay on a steel table, having his face sewn up. I looked at the pile of clothes on the floor, filthy and bloody with tiny sparkles of glass in them. I wished someone had thrown them away.

Gene and I walked over to Jeremy. He was covered in a clean white sheet and his neck was encased in a soft brace. An ER doctor patiently stitched up a gash in his forehead. It was deep, about seven inches long, and ran right through his left eyebrow. Without taking his eyes off his work, the doctor said matter-of-factly, "Jeremy has a broken right hip and two bad fractures in his left femur. A surgeon is on the way. He'll operate immediately. If everything goes well, he'll be out of surgery by one A.M."

Gene sat down in a nearby chair, but I stood by the table. Jeremy's eyes met mine slowly. He hadn't been able to look me in the eye for long months now. His bloody, dirty hand crept out from under the sheet and reached for mine. "Mama, I'm—I'm—

going to make you and Gene proud of me yet. You'll see. I love you. Where's Gene?"

Gene stood quickly and put his hand on top of ours. "I love you too, Jeremy, and I'm proud of you," I said.

Jeremy's eyes met Gene's. "I love you, Jeremy," Gene said.

A harried nurse rushed into the room. "Doctor," she said, "we need you in rooms five and three."

The doctor kept stitching methodically. "Can't let anyone else do this. Too deep," he said.

When Jeremy was taken to surgery, Gene and I went to wait in the empty surgical waiting room. We knew Jeremy would be in the hospital a few days, but then what? Where would he live? He couldn't return to his house, which looked as though it had been trashed by a gang of vandals. Unable to walk, he was going to require care, long-term care. Jeremy had lived with us for three months a while back, after his second admission to the behavioral facility. He began lying to us and inhaling an aerosol sold to clean sound equipment. It gives the user a high, and it can't be traced through blood or urine. It also does horrible stomach damage. We'd taken Jeremy to the ER twice throwing up blood and desperately sick. Insisting he was fine, he had gone back to his house.

Jeremy had started a landscaping business fifteen years ago, and he had built it into a fine company. All his customers, from little old ladies to nice-sized businesses, were very pleased with Jeremy's quick, efficient work. He also had a part-time job with a company where he'd worked for fourteen years without missing a day. He owned stock in the company, had a nice savings account and a house that would soon be paid for. He kept meticulous books and managed his money well.

That was before he trusted a friend to do his bookkeeping. In less than two years everything was gone, and he was more than two hundred thousand dollars in debt.

When the truth sank in, he started taking something to help him sleep. And he started to use recreational drugs. Lots of his friends took them. He began missing work at the company where his record had been perfect. He stayed in bed for days. He didn't eat. He stopped answering his phone and his pager. He shut out all his relatives. His world got smaller and stranger until he was confined to his house, without electricity and water. He was dirty and hungry. Sometimes he made trips to a nearby grocery store and accepted the food the nice ladies who worked there offered. He didn't pay his yard-maintenance helpers, and they started sitting on his front porch. His customers called me, wanting to know why Jeremy hadn't shown up to do their yards. He accumulated all kinds of junk in his yard and on his front porch—strange things, like chunks of granite, beat-up ladders, blinds for an entire house, scrap metal. His mail, including overdue bills, piled up unopened.

The friend eased out of the picture and Jeremy didn't press charges. "I'm to blame too," he insisted. The doctors thought the trauma of losing so much he'd worked so hard for had pushed him over the edge.

For months, Gene and I tried to help him. His house was locked and he didn't answer the door. I wasn't certain he was alive. All his vehicles were there, including his work trucks, so we knew he was inside.

One day we went over to his house and walked around it to his bedroom window. I took the screen down and knocked loudly on the window, which was right by his bed. "Jeeeeeremy!" I shouted.

After about five minutes, he appeared suddenly on the cluttered front porch in his underwear. He hadn't shaved for days, and his beautiful red hair was long and dirty. He squinted in the bright sunshine, all skin and bones. He was unsteady on his feet and obviously in a rage.

Right now you have to stay calm, Marion. Move slowly. Speak softly. Smile a bit. Be a mother. Remember when he was a tiny baby and you bathed and powdered him? Remember how he loved to laugh? Remember how he nearly died when he was just nine months old, and the doctors said that most babies couldn't have survived and that he was a strong, determined little fellow? Remember when he thought before the rest of us that his father might have a terminal illness, and he offered to quit school and go to work and provide for the family? Remember how he took over the huge yard when his daddy couldn't stand, much less cut the grass? And he never stopped taking care of it. One morning he was cutting it at 4:00 A.M. because he had plans for the day. Remember how he worked all summer when he was only twelve and saved every penny because he wanted a brand new go-cart? Remember the day his daddy took him to downtown Atlanta, and Jeremy paid for the bright blue go-cart—a hundred and thirteen dollars? Remember how he came tearing through the house yelling, "Mama, Mama! Come see it!"

He's that same person now—and he's hurting terribly. He's bottled up his feelings for so long. Help me, Lord. Help me do what Jeremy needs me to do now.

Just then Jeremy leaned over the banister and screamed, "Go away! I don't need you, Mother. Leave me alone. Don't you hear me? I have to sleep. Get off my property!"

Oh, Jeremy, let me help you. I ran up the front steps and said, simply, "Hi."

He started bellowing all over again. "Why are you here? Get off my property! Why did you take down my screen? I'll call the police if you don't leave now."

He ran into the house and tried to slam the door, but I eased inside. When I tried to hug him he threw up his arms, and I knew if I didn't back off, he'd probably shove me. I stepped back. *How am I able to do this?*

I'm helping you, Marion, I thought God said. *Leave now. Gently and quietly.* And so Gene and I did the unthinkable. We got into our car and drove off. It felt as if a part of me were staying there—holding Jeremy, soothing him.

A few months later during a lucid time, when Jeremy was taking the medicine the psychiatrist had prescribed, he remembered that day, speaking softly, almost as if it had happened to someone else.

"I had no idea when I'd bathed or shaved. I'd been in bed about three days. I made it dark in here so I could sleep and not think. I hated the light, but I hated the darkness too. I hated being alone, and I hated being with people. I hated the thought of asking for help, and I couldn't imagine continuing without it.

"I remember that I was constantly fighting with the bed covers—they were a huge snarled ball. Someone kept screaming my name and banging on the window. I knew it had to be you. No one else would be so persistent. I couldn't get untangled from the sheets to get out of bed. They wouldn't let go of me. Finally, I escaped and leaped out of bed so angry I scared myself.

"I kicked at the filthy clothes, muddy shoes, stale food, and wet towels on the floor. I didn't even know or care if I had clothes on. I almost stumbled running into the living room. The floor was covered with all kinds of junk: business papers, magazines, shoes, fast-food containers, empty cereal boxes, drink cans, unopened bank statements and bills, more dirty clothes. I unlocked the front door, flung it open, shoved aside battered boxes full of some of the "deals" I'd bought.

"My thoughts were racing so fast I couldn't process them. *You're messed up financially. You're gonna lose your house. You're stupid, and you'll always be stupid. You're not like everyone else. Nobody likes you; God doesn't even care about you. Loser!*

"I remember thinking that you were poking your nose in my business. When I tried to shut you out and you slipped through the front door, I hated you."

He stopped talking and looked at me. "I know . . . but we aren't there now, are we?" I asked. I wanted him to keep talking. It seemed like poison was draining from him.

"I thought if I screamed gutter talk and foul language that you'd get mad and leave. Fuss back, something. But you just stood there, smiling your pathetic little smile and holding out your skinny hands. I could see Gene outside on the porch. I screamed so loud that my throat hurt, and I never let myself look into your eyes.

"You and Gene left and I crawled back into that filthy bed, full of cracker crumbs, dirt off my boots, old banana peels, all kinds of trash. I curled up under the blanket and cried, realizing how desperately I needed you and Gene. Squirming around in bed, I kept on crying, hating the sounds I made but hating silence too. Hating everything and everyone—especially myself."

Jeremy stopped talking, and we sat quietly. I have a habit of talking too much, analyzing things way too much, asking too many questions. But that day God told me, *Leave him alone. Be still and be quiet.*

So I said, "Thank you, Jeremy. That was brave. Why don't you go rest until supper is ready?" Looking relieved, he went back to the bedroom he used at our house.

It was a little after one in the morning when the surgeon found Gene and me in the small waiting room. He told us that Jeremy's surgery had gone well and that we'd talk later.

He was alive. He'd survived four car wrecks in a matter of weeks, and other dangers I could only imagine. He was sleeping now. Not hurting, mentally or physically. I liked thinking about that. I couldn't think about what to do when he woke up—what kind of plans to make, where to get help for him. My mind was unable to function clearly anymore. For so many years I'd lived with fear of the future; I didn't have the energy now. All I could do was hang on for the moment. We had to get home and get some sleep—so we could get up and deal with what tomorrow might bring.

We got back home around three that morning. The next day we'd just returned from visiting Jeremy when the phone rang. I answered and listened, not believing what I heard. It was another urgent voice from another hospital. "You need to get here now. Your son Jon has been admitted and is in critical condition. We aren't certain about the diagnosis."

We found Jon in a private room, burning up with fever and on morphine for pain. He lay very still in the hospital bed, wearing the red checkered boxer shorts I'd given him for Christmas. "We're waiting for a hand surgeon," he mumbled, not opening his eyes. His right hand was so thickly bandaged that he seemed to be wearing a boxing glove. "What happened?" Gene asked softly.

"A tiny nick on my finger . . . got infected. There are red marks going all the way up to my shoulder. Hurts like . . ."

Five hours later the surgeon arrived from another emergency surgery at a hospital across town. He talked to us after Jon's surgery. "Your son is very sick. He's being admitted to intensive care. This is life-threatening. He could lose fingers, his hand, part of his arm. You've probably never heard of necrotizing fasciitis. It's very rare. Powerful bacteria enter the body and quickly destroy the soft tissue just beneath the skin. That's why they call it the flesh-eating disease. I suspect that's what Jon has. We'll have to wait for lab reports and cultures. I'll have to do more surgery while he's here and keep him on something strong for the pain."

Gene moved closer and put his arm around me. I made myself say, "Do you know he's addicted to drugs?"

The doctor didn't answer my question. "He has to have something for the pain. Here's my beeper number," he said as he handed us a card. "Call me if you have questions."

Jon was hospitalized for eleven days. He had five surgeries, the last one a skin graft using skin from his thigh. He didn't complain much; he joked with everyone in the hospital—just like his father Jerry had when they discovered he was suffering from a brain tumor. Everyone had adored Jerry, and now, almost twenty years later, the staff—even the physicians—liked and admired Jon.

Gene and I spent most of our time and energy driving from one hospital to the other; they were about forty minutes apart. We explained to each of my sons how the other was doing. They'd never seemed very close—they argued a lot—but now each one talked openly about his brother and how he loved him. They phoned each other, laughing, joking, amazed that somehow they were both in the hospital, each wanting to see the other.

By the second day, I had no idea what day or even month it was. Everything seemed unreal. I was numb, but sensed that fear was planning a sudden attack. I felt that I could endure anything but fear. Before crawling into bed that night, I pulled out a poem I'd written when Jerry was taking chemotherapy:

THE CHOICE

We have to make a choice
To live in despair
Or joy
To walk in fear
Or in faith
To dwell under the shadow of the Almighty
Or reside in open spaces of self-effort
There's no in-between place
No halfway house
It's one way or the other
Pity for ourselves
Or compassion for others
Loneliness
Or reaching out
Joy and happiness are not even related
Joy springs from deep within
And has nothing to do with circumstances
Jesus promised us His joy
Happiness comes from without
Through things, people, desires fulfilled
Help me, Father, for I have made a choice

Not based on emotion
I have chosen to reject despair, fear and finally
Self-pity
Looking to You alone . . .
Oh, Father, already I sense the joy that comes
From the agonizing choice I made.

Father, I have a choice to make tonight. As tired as I am, and with this fear running through me, I still have a choice. I don't feel like I do; I feel backed into a corner, and I'd like to sit down in that corner and feel sorry for myself. Instead, I'm going to choose to look to You alone. Tonight, right now, I again choose to reject despair and self-pity and fear. With Habakkuk, I will fix my heart on You.

JON'S DECISION | 2

WHILE GENE AND I and Jon and Jeremy's sisters, Julie and Jennifer, and our pastor waited through Jon's third surgery, my mind drifted back two years to the May evening when Jon had finally come to Gene and me to ask for help with his addictions.

Jon had brought steaks from the butcher shop he managed and grilled them for us. He was smiling and laughing as though he didn't have a problem in the world, wanting to know how we had liked the steaks. "Did I cook 'em perfect or what?"

Afterward he settled down in our brown swivel recliner, moving it back and forth, staring at the ceiling. At six feet two inches and two hundred pounds, he was actually too large for the chair. Gene went into the kitchen to finish up the dishes; I sat on the sofa studying Jon. He seemed to be struggling to say something difficult.

"What is it, Jon?" I finally asked, never one for patience in anything.

He was silent for maybe a minute. Then he said, "I'm ready for help. God told me that you and Gene would help me."

Gene overheard him and hurried into the living room. He sat down by me, leaning toward Jon with his hands clasped between his knees. "It's time, Jon, and if you're serious, we want to help you."

We knew about a place that might be able to help Jon— Dunklin Memorial Camp, located in the middle of nowhere on a hundred and forty swampy acres in Central Florida. Run by former addicts, Dunklin could accommodate seventy-five men. There was always a waiting list. A man had to be desperate to get into Dunklin—he had to beg to be admitted to the nine-month program.

A close physician friend of ours, whose own son was at Dunklin, had told us that if Jon didn't get help soon. . . . He left the sentence unfinished, but we knew. This was a life-or-death situation.

Dunklin seemed like a good possibility for Jon, but there were obstacles. Jon would have to quit his job, get out of a lease on the house he shared with another guy, and then humble himself and beg to be admitted. He'd have to admit his desperation to a stranger, on the phone.

The next day I phoned Gene from my car to tell him I was running late shopping. "Marion," he interrupted, "Jon just phoned. He's quit his job. He's on his way here."

When I arrived home, sure enough, Jon's big white Chevy truck was out front. I couldn't help but smile at it. I wanted to run up and hug it and say, "Thank you, truck, for bringing Jon here."

After supper that night, Jon finally got around to making that phone call to Dunklin. *He's looking pretty cocky,* I thought as he went into my office to use the phone. When he came out fifteen minutes later, he looked stunned. "Some jerk named David doesn't believe I'm desperate or sincere. He said to think about it some more and call him back tomorrow." Jon pounded on the kitchen table, "What else do they want from me?" he said. Then he walked out of the house, climbed into his truck, and roared off.

The next day Jon was back, looking like a little boy uncertain about what to do. I could sense a quiet rebellion underneath his jokes. I was afraid I'd say the wrong thing to him, so I went into the bedroom, lay down on the bed, and went to sleep. As I drifted off, I heard Jon phoning David again.

David wasn't available, Jon told us later, and didn't return his call for five hours. When he did call, he said, "Jon, why should I let you have this bed when twenty other men want it? Think some more and call me back."

"I don't have to take this crap!" Jon bellowed to no one in particular. Even in my disappointment, I liked David. He knew how to play hardball. When Jon roared off again in his truck, I felt like he'd taken my hope with him.

He returned on Saturday. *Don't nag or offer advice. Don't question him. You're asking for a fight if you do. Let Gene and Jon talk. Get out of the picture.* Once again I sought escape through a nap. I heard Jon asking Gene, "Where's Mom?" Gene told him and I heard Jon walking to the bedroom. I tried to look sound asleep. He stalked into the bedroom and leaned hard against the bedpost, shaking the bed.

When I didn't stir, he said, "I think I can get my old job back."

"Mmm," I answered.

"A nine-month program is too long anyway."

"Umm," I said and half yawned.

Jon yawned. "Man, I'm tired."

I bit. "Why?"

"Did cocaine last night. Wears me out."

I clenched my teeth in order not to respond. Through the years I'd come up with twenty-two plans to get Jon on the right track. Fine plans. None had worked. I wasn't going to be able to help my son. I stared at the ceiling, replying in a monotone. "That right?"

"Well, I'm going to see some of my friends," he said curtly. "Maybe I'll be back to go to church with y'all tomorrow."

Jon liked our little church. He admired our minister, Jerry Varnado, a former Georgia Bulldogs football player who quit a successful law practice when he met up with Jesus. Jon's father had adored the Bulldogs, and so did Jon and Jeremy. Jon didn't know that everyone in our church, from seven-year-old Avie to eighty-year-old Roque, prayed for him daily.

"Bye, Jon," I managed, still staring hopelessly at the ceiling. *Lord, he belongs to You, not me. Put Your angels of protection around him. Help me sleep.*

I'd almost finished dressing the next morning when the phone rang. Gene answered it in the kitchen. I tried to smile at myself in the mirror, hoping to look normal. I grabbed my Bible and walked into the kitchen to meet Gene. He stood with his hand still on the phone, head bowed. He looked up slowly, "It was Jon. He's on his way and asked that we wait for him. I have to be at church early today. Can you wait?"

"Of course," I answered, trying to sound matter-of-fact, while blinking rapidly to keep the tears from smearing my mascara. A verse from Romans slipped into my dancing heart. *Hope does not disappoint.*

A few minutes later, the white truck roared up the driveway. Jon was showered and shaved, wearing khaki pants and a new white shirt. As we drove to church I reached out to tune the car radio to my favorite Christian station. But then I pulled my hand back. I wasn't going to do one single thing. No matter what the outcome, it would have to be all God, not Mama.

We arrived at the little white church and found a parking spot. I'd seen some powerful prayers answered in this place.

We were singing praise songs toward the end of the service and I hadn't even glanced Jon's way. I felt numb. But then a thought came: *Get ready for a hug.* I reasoned it was my overactive imagination, because my Jon would never show emotion. So I continued singing, looking straight ahead. Suddenly I was seized in a grip so hard that I could barely breathe.

Jon! My Jon nearly hugged the life out of me. I hugged him back and we clung together tightly. "Mom, go to the altar with me," Jon said. *Hope does not disappoint.*

In our church, people go to the altar pretty regularly. There are even boxes of tissues for the inevitable tears. Jon and I found a place to kneel at the altar. There were others kneeling there. Gene was already there praying with someone.

"Mom, pray for me."

I prayed softly, wondering, *Is this really happening—after all these years?* Pastor Jerry came over and placed his huge football-player's hands on Jon's head and began praying boldly, claiming Jon for God's will and purpose. Then Gene was there with his arms around both of us, and I saw and felt others close by, their arms and hands, their voices softly thanking God. Jon was crying and laughing and thanking everyone—broken.

Back home, Jon wanted to talk. "I believe my healing began at church," he said joyfully. "Man, what a church! What love! I'm going to call David again. He *has* to let me come to Dunklin now." He was holding the phone in one hand and David's number in the other when the phone rang.

"Hello," Jon answered, still smiling. Suddenly, his face lit up, and he started laughing. "Really?" he said, then "Thank you, buddy," over and over again. He hung up the phone. "Mom, they want me!" he said, so low and tenderly I could barely hear him. "David has a bed for me. He said God told them I was . . . broken. I get to go to Dunklin, Mom."

Our living room seemed full of delirious hope as Jon and I hugged in a long, fierce embrace, rocking back and forth, both of us crying, not even trying to control our loud sobs of relief and joy. *Oh, God, after seventeen years, it's really going to happen. Jon's getting help.* I could hardly breathe or think or function; intense joy can be as overwhelming as intense pain.

The whole family gathered on our deck the next afternoon: Jeremy and Jon, their sisters Julie and Jennifer and their husbands and my six grandchildren. We had homemade ice cream and Julie made a pound cake. It felt just like Christmas on Memorial Day.

Julie, Gene and I took Jon to the Atlanta airport early the next morning to catch a flight to West Palm Beach. Jon boarded the plane looking as though he might be going on vacation to fish and golf in Florida as he had done many times before. Just before he disappeared from sight, he turned and looked back at us. He was smiling, but his smile was a cautious one. He'd looked exactly like that on his first day of school, when he boarded the school bus with Jeremy. We took pictures of everything that morning, and when the plane took off, we looked straight up in the air and snapped a picture of it—flying Jon to Dunklin to be set free.

Oh, Father, You're on the plane with him, I know You are! I don't know how to praise You enough for what's happening. I don't think I've ever seen the sky so blue. My heart is about to burst with joy! Thank You, thank You.

DUNKLIN | 3

TWO WEEKS LATER, a letter arrived from Jon. I stood at the mailbox examining the stamp, his handwriting, and the postmark, and then I ran to the house shouting for Gene. We read the letter together on the sofa:

June 10, 2001

Hey, Mother, Gene, Julie, Jeremy, Jennifer:

Can you believe that God had me sit by a lady on the plane whose son had graduated from Dunklin? Am I in God's plan or what? Y'all can't imagine how powerful the presence of the Holy Spirit is here and in me. I've only just started my program and the rest of my life. How strong will I be twenty years from now! The Lord has already done more miracles here, not only in me, but all around me, than I can remember! His miracles still amaze me, though.

Feel free to come whenever you want to, just write me and let me know. Joy like you have never experienced will flood each of your souls when you come. The Lord is going to pour out blessings on our family like you can't imagine. It's not easy though—there are problems here too, but they're immediately solved by getting together with a brother and openly praying about them.

Jeremy, I love you so much, and I love each of you. Anyone who comes here will be blessed without measure, and you can tell who's really writing this: the Holy Spirit, so you know it's true. Nothing like walking in obedience! Could write forever and ever and probably shouldn't stop because I can really feel the Lord's presence over my letter. But if I don't stop now, I never will.

A new guy came into the program about four days after me. He's twenty-three. Mother and father deceased, can't track down any family members. Made a living out of hustling people. Overdosed four times on heroin and speed. Had to have Narcon injections and paddle shock each time. He came to Dunklin to hide out from dealers he had robbed. He had no knowledge of the Lord. God let me love him. He's a born-again believer now and prays for y'all daily with me. Well, I'm crying now, but from joy. *Be ready when you come!* The Spirit of Jesus is very powerful here. Can't believe this letter. Got to stop writing. Past time to turn lights off. Lots of rules. Can't wait for your response. How much more joy by the time I'm thirty-four? For everyone in our family?

So sorry for missed family time before. We'll make it up, Mom, don't cry now. Gene, your family is going to be all right too. Thus sayeth the LORD!

Love, Jon

There were more letters. Sometimes I couldn't see them through my tears. All the men in the program worked hard, starting early, and they also attended classes on inner healing, restoration, making things right with those they'd hurt, being "in

Christ," and all the good stuff I'd ever wanted for Jon. He started off in their wood mill, like most newcomers, but soon became the camp's official butcher. At Dunklin Memorial Camp the "brothers" grow their own vegetables, harvest them, cook the meals, and clean the kitchen. Jon's job was to furnish the meat, starting with live cows and pigs. He hadn't wanted to have to shoot an animal, but he'd told me before leaving, "I'll do whatever they tell me to do." They also harvested oranges and shipped them all over the U.S.

And Dunklin Memorial Church was on the campsite, with the congregation coming from all around, loving the men in the program as though they were their own sons—their own prodigal sons—being restored.

Jon couldn't use the phone, not even to call us. He wasn't allowed newspapers or television or radio. The guys had a little pocket money from working at their assigned jobs. When the canteen opened—twice a week, for thirty minutes—the line formed instantly, with lots of good-humored laughter and encouraging talk between the brothers. They were allowed to spend two dollars on Popsicles, candy bars, soda, and ice cream sandwiches.

The men came from all walks of life. When we first visited, one arrived fresh from Wall Street, another from sleeping in a box under a New York bridge. They were tough-looking men until you looked into their eyes. Then you saw love, repentance, even joy and hope. They had been given another chance at life.

The men learned to have daily quiet time early in the morning while it was still cool. They prayed alone and then wrote in their prayer journals; they listened for God to speak and wrote what they thought He said to them. When Jon first showed me his journal, a stenographer's pad, I asked him, "Why did you write on the front and back, son?"

"That's the rules, Mom," he said, smiling. "We're taught not to waste anything here."

I'd never known Jon to be so happy, despite the rules, the extremely hard work, the heat and the pain of looking back at his life to discover the reason for his addictions. He had to face some incredible emotional pain.

Many men lived clean after Dunklin, but not all of them. The very week Jon got there, he was asked to be a pallbearer for a man who had graduated the program, but died of an overdose soon after his release. They had the funeral there at Dunklin Memorial Church with the man's wife and their two babies in attendance. Jon said all the men cried and prayed for the new widow, surrounding her with love.

At summer's end Gene and I, this time with Julie, Jeremy, and Jennifer, flew down to visit Jon. At supper our first evening there, Jon stood and introduced us to the men, and we got a huge round of applause. The mess hall was rustic, plain, large—built to serve its purpose. For years the floor had been dirt; now the guys and the staff were proud of their new floors and kept them swept clean.

The men—tired, hungry men who'd been working in the sweltering heat all day—motioned for us to go on ahead of them. The men had grown the food, harvested it, butchered the meat, and cooked it. It was beautifully displayed, buffet-style, and those with kitchen duty stood beaming behind the table. Jon introduced us to so many men that we couldn't keep their names straight. Each one shook hands with us and gave us an unforgettable smile.

Jon chose a spot for us, and we all sat down at a long table. The blessing and Bible reading were given by one of the brothers.

I'd never heard the Bible read with such desperation or dedication. When we opened our eyes, Julie's were brimming with tears. Jennifer started sobbing and fled from the dining hall.

"It happens," Jon explained matter-of-factly.

"I've never been in a room so full of love," Julie said. Jeremy concentrated on his food and asked where the ketchup was. Jon hopped up quickly to get it for him. I had to remember all the ketchup fights they'd had when they were youngsters. They could argue about anything!

Julie went outside to check on Jennifer, and Jon said, "The first night they introduced me here as the new guy, everyone stood and applauded. I was so scared I could hardly stand up. Then some of them came over and hugged me, not a polite little greeting, but a long, hard hug. We all hug here and cry together. It's like nothing I've ever experienced."

Jeremy didn't really seem to like anyone there—except Laura Mae. Forty-two years ago, her husband Mickey and another young man had knelt in what was to become Dunklin Memorial Camp and asked God to give him the place to set addicts free. Mickey and Laura Mae had lived on the grounds ever since. Laura Mae hadn't taken to the place at first; when Mickey showed her the wilderness, a snake wrapped itself around her leg. Now she wasn't surprised by anything.

After supper, Mickey, a huge, smiling man who looked like a Texas rancher, came over and hugged all of us. "Jon," he said, "bring your family over to the dock after supper and we'll feed the koi fish."

Jeremy smiled at last. He'd built some koi ponds for customers; this was a much more comfortable subject for him than addictions and rules and emotions.

By the time we left Dunklin, we'd grown close to many of

Jon's friends. He'd been right about the love at Dunklin: No one's an outsider there; everyone is included. Everyone is loved.

Back home, sometimes it was hard to contain all the joy—just thinking about Jon at Dunklin made me rejoice. His letters came regularly. There were no complaints. He did write an urgent note as the weather got hotter: "Mom, send lots of Kool-Aid. We're playing ball, and we drink it by the gallon."

I nearly bought out the grocery store. I packed the Kool-Aid with a letter and drove with Gene to the UPS office. He shook his head, smiling to himself.

"What?" I asked.

"Nothing."

"Tell me!"

"I can't help but laugh. Only Jon could have gone from cocaine to Kool-Aid with such apparent ease."

Father, You know there was a time when I wouldn't have put one foot in a place like this. Thank You for the beauty all around me—the healing, the compassion, even the brokenness. I am so blessed to be here and to meet these men. Thank You that Jon's here!

AN UNEXPECTED | 4
CHRISTMAS

As the holidays approached that year, I felt a kind of dread. It would be my first Christmas without my mother, who'd died in July. And Jon wouldn't be with us. Everyone in the family had always come to my house for Christmas dinner. Around the first of December, Gene asked me what was wrong. "I guess I don't feel much like celebrating," I said.

"I know," he said, "Maybe we could do something different this year."

I didn't reply. But as the weather got colder and stores played Christmas carols and I saw Christmas cards displayed, the dread became almost overwhelming. One evening Gene said, "What would you think about spending Christmas at Dunklin with Jon?"

"You'd do that?" I said. We usually didn't travel at Christmas. We didn't even know if we could get plane reservations that close to the holidays. It seemed impossible—like running away. No turkey to cook, no goodies to bake, no tree, no gift wrapping, no Christmas cards to address. *Would it still be like Christmas in that swamp so far away from home?*

"I think we're supposed to go," Gene said firmly. Jeremy, Julie, Jennifer and the grandchildren were happy that Jon wouldn't be alone and urged us to do it.

Two days before Christmas, we drove the last few desolate

miles through the tunnel of live oaks. Towering high above the car, they blocked out the sky and our lingering Christmas regrets.

At Dunklin, Gene parked in the shade, and we spotted Jon standing near the door of the mess hall with some of the brothers. It was lunch time.

Don't holler to him or run over there or do anything weird or overly motherly now.

Jon was talking and laughing, using his hands as he spoke. I was certain he saw us, so I waited for him to run over to us. But he kept talking. It wasn't Jon who rushed over; it was Errol.

When Jon introduced us to Errol on our previous trip to Dunklin, our eyes met and I reached out and hugged him like a son. He hugged me back. Errol had left the program three times. He was from nearby, but had been living in a box under a bridge in New York. Except for the glow in his eyes, he looked hard—streetwise. He was skinny, with sharp tanned features and a crew cut. Somehow he'd hung onto to an incredible sense of humor. When I first met him, his mother wasn't speaking to him. She wouldn't accept his letters or even the dozen yellow roses he'd sent her for Mother's Day. Every day he searched through the mail for a letter from her. There never was one. Even though Errol smiled and joked a lot, his expression betrayed the pain he still bore. I'd been writing short notes to Errol since our first meeting.

He had almost reached our car, running like a ballplayer rounding third base, when he stopped suddenly, turned, and looked back at Jon. Jon strolled slowly toward us. After Gene and I had hugged Jon, Errol sprinted over to us and hugged us. He was amazingly strong. "Hey, Fatso," I teased.

"I've gained thirty pounds," he bragged, patting his lean torso.

"You look great, Errol!" I said. He was smiling, but there was still pain in his eyes. Standing there under palm trees with lush flowering shrubs around us and the Florida sun beaming down, it didn't seem like Christmas, but I didn't mind.

I asked Errol to sit at our table for lunch. "How are you, really?" I asked him.

"I'm making real progress. I'm finally beginning to believe that it wasn't my fault that my brother . . . killed himself. Even though Mom doesn't answer my letters yet, it could happen." He looked away briefly.

"It will, Errol. Let's believe it will," I answered.

Because it was Christmas, the men nearing graduation would be allowed to leave the camp with supervision. We planned to take Jon and some of his friends out to eat. This would be Jon's first time off the grounds of Dunklin since he'd arrived in May.

Occasionally, some of the guys will decide that the program's too tough and walk away. They're free to do that. But they must wait three full months before applying for re-entry. Errol had run away three times, but he'd stuck it out this time and would be graduating with Jon's class.

I could almost understand why some left. The inner healing process is said to be particularly uncomfortable. The brothers call it "inner screaming." With the help of counselors who've been through the program themselves, the addict returns emotionally to that place in time when he could no longer face his feelings. For Jon, his father's death when he was fifteen was that place.

Errol interrupted my thoughts. "What do you think of our Christmas tree, Mrs. West? We decorated the mess hall all by ourselves."

I looked intently at the tall cedar tree with packages underneath and the bright twinkling lights strung around the room and the red and green paper streamers. "It looks . . . just like Christmas, Errol!"

The next day, as we got ready for our lunchtime outing, Jon said, "Y'all knew Steve was going with us, but I hope it's okay—I invited Errol. You should have seen his face light up. It'll be a little crowded, but we won't mind."

I was overjoyed. Gene and I got into the front seats of our small rented car, and Jon and Steve got in the back.

Errol was outside his quarters sitting on a fence when we drove by. He came running over even before Gene stopped the car. "Hey, guys, thanks for inviting me. I'll just squeeze in here in the middle since I'm the smallest." Jon and Steve made room for him in the backseat. At the steakhouse, the three men took their time studying the menu before they ordered.

The staff had given each man a twenty-five-dollar Wal-Mart gift certificate—a contribution from a nearby church—so on Christmas Eve afternoon Gene and I took Jon, Errol and Steve out shopping. As we split up in the large store, I could see Errol heading for the Christmas cards.

It was turning downright cold, so I looked around for a warmer shirt. I found a bright red one marked down to nearly nothing and bought it.

Back in the car Jon showed us his new shoes. Steve had bought a shirt. "Look, everybody, at what I bought!" Errol said, leaning forward from the backseat and showing Gene and me the small gold cross he'd already placed around his neck. "I've never had one before. I never even understood what the cross meant—but I do now!"

By nightfall it had turned so cold that it felt just like Christmas. The stars seemed lower, larger, even brighter against a black-velvet sky. We joined the brothers and the other visiting families around a huge bonfire. One of the men strummed a guitar as we gazed into the fire.

The next morning was chilly, so I put on three shirts, the new red one on the outside. Then around mid-morning, without warning, I developed an overwhelming craving for chocolate. Because I knew civilization was twenty miles away, I started to panic. Jon, Gene and I were sitting on the beds in our motel room, thankful for the heat. "Jon," I finally blurted out, "I'm having a chocolate fit. Could you try to find me just one piece of candy?"

"You sound like an addict, Mom," Jon said. He left the room laughing and called out, "Don't get your hopes up."

After a while I heard Jon's familiar unhurried walk as he approached our room. He came in and dropped a small paper bag in my lap. I opened it hopefully. *Two chocolate bars!* "Oh, Jon, I don't think I've ever wanted anything so much in my life. Thanks a million." I devoured one of the bars silently, gratefully. I was about to open the second when Jon asked, "Aren't you going to read the card, Mom?"

Card? I peeked back in the sack and pulled out an envelope. I didn't recognize the neat handwriting. It said, "Gene and Marion." There were hearts drawn under our names. The front of the card read,

Through the days of December
God's love and blessings
are the best things to remember.

Inside, it continued,

One of His special blessings is having friends like you.
Have a very special Christmas season.
"I bring you good news of great joy that
will be for all people" (Luke 2:10).

Below were a few lines of very neat handwriting.

Dear Gene and Marion,
     I do appreciate everything you have done to make this
holiday so very special. God Bless!
                                        Love, Errol

Suddenly, I couldn't even taste the chocolate.

Jon said, "He bought y'all the card at Wal-Mart, and also four candy bars. Two was all he had left, but he was *so* excited to give them to you, Mom. There was no talking him out of it."

There in that motel room in the middle of a swamp, twenty-five miles from anywhere, wearing my new seven-dollar red shirt, the very spirit of Christmas escaped from a Wal-Mart sack and found me. Here at Dunklin, I'd run right into the heart of it.

Father, don't ever let me forget this Christmas. Stay close to Errol. Help him make it here. Help Jon too—help all these beautiful, broken men become whole.

A TRUCKLOAD | 5
OF ANGELS |

I WAS BACK IN THE HOSPITAL AGAIN, sitting in the surgical waiting room while Jon went through another operation on his hand. I'd never have thought that I'd be able to sit and wait through five surgeries in one ghastly hospital stay.

As a young mother, I'd nearly gone off the deep end when one of my children had routine surgery. I'd wanted to go into the operating room for four-year-old Jennifer's tonsillectomy. Every moment she'd been gone was agony; over and over I imagined the doctor walking toward me grim-faced, maybe even crying, saying something like, "It shouldn't have happened . . ." It never entered my mind to imagine him bouncing down the hall, smiling, saying, "Everything went beautifully. She's in recovery. You can see her. . . ." And that's exactly what happened. But back then, I always imagined the worst.

Now, as I waited for Jon's surgeon to come to the waiting room, other images filled my mind, memories of Jon and Jeremy and a truckload of angels. . . .

It was two years after Jerry's death. Jon and Jeremy, then seventeen, and I fought daily. It was as though I lived with two King Kongs. Many nights they wouldn't show up for supper, or even call. I'd sit at the old oak kitchen table alone, unable to eat, wondering what trouble they might be getting into. On weekends they stayed out until way past their curfew. When they finally got home, I could sometimes smell beer beneath the gum they chewed to sweeten their breath. And what kind of girls were calling at three in the morning, refusing to give their names when I answered the phone?

That night I'd prepared their favorite foods, roast beef with potatoes, carrots and fresh green beans, rolls and gingerbread. I stood at the stove stirring the gravy. *Not one lump!* I congratulated myself and set down the wooden spoon when the phone rang.

"Hi, Mom," Jeremy said. "Brian's mom invited me to stay and eat." Brian lived down the street. "They're grilling hamburgers, like we. . . ."

Like we used to do when we were a real family, I filled in silently. "Okay, Jeremy. Thanks for calling." As I hung the kitchen phone back on the wall, I heard Jon's truck thunder into the driveway. *Maybe he'll walk in smiling. Maybe we'll even get along, like family.* I decided to try to do my part and be calm and cheerful, interested in whatever he talked about.

Jon marched into the kitchen, his face grim, set, determined. *Here we go.* I looked down at the green beans cooking on low. "Hi, Jon. Supper's almost ready." The words weren't angry, but my tone was hardly "mother of the year."

"I'm not hungry," Jon said, "Anyway, I'm going to a party. And don't hassle me, okay?"

Thoughts of one of those parties with the beer, girls and who-knows-what-else made my mouth go dry. I kept my voice steady, though. "I'd hoped you would stay home tonight."

"I *said* I'm going out."

"Look, I cooked a roast," I announced, lifting the lid.

"Mom, I'm going!" Jon bellowed.

I slammed the top back on the pot, nearly knocking it off the stove and glared at him. "No! No! No!" I screamed. "You are not!"

"How are you going to stop me?" he taunted.

I looked around. It looked like a kitchen. It smelled like a kitchen. But it had become an ugly battleground—again. I followed Jon to the door and stood in front of it, facing him. I folded my arms across my chest and planted my feet firmly, wishing I weren't wearing an apron.

Jon looked stunned for a second, all six feet two inches of him. He weighed two hundred pounds, an athlete in top physical shape. He gently slipped his hands under my elbows, lifted me a few inches off the ground and moved me out of the doorway. Then he set me down again.

I rushed after him, fighting the panic welling up inside of me. I would have to lie awake alone in the dark, still house, waiting, wondering, listening. I wasn't sure I could do it again tonight. Jon stood in the doorway, hesitating. His big frame filled it entirely. He was even taller than his father.

Then Jon was gone.

I didn't run ahead of him and grab the keys from his beloved green truck as I'd done before. Once, when he headed out for a Friday-night party, I'd gotten them and thrown them into a field behind our house. Desperate people do foolish things.

Jon settled into the driver's seat and leaned out the window to adjust the mirror. *I'm not going to become a begging, sniffling wimp of a mother tonight! Help me, Lord. You promised to be a husband to widows. Be mine now.* Jon raced the motor victoriously. He wore that cocky, nobody-can-stop-me-now expression that I hated.

Without fanfare a Scripture came into my mind: *"Are there not ministering angels?"* A surge of excitement ran through me.

"Jon," I called out, smiling as darkness closed in and the street-lights blinked on.

Still in the driveway, he hit the brakes hard and leaned out the window, "Yeah?" He was sure he'd won.

"I just wanted to say good-bye, son. And one more thing: I'm putting angels in the back of your truck." I turned quickly to go inside. As I stepped through the door, I heard the squeal of his brakes again. What a marvelous, beautiful sound!

"Mom! Mom!"

I turned slowly, casually, I hoped. The ball was in my court now. "Yes, Jon?"

"Can you—*do* that?"

"Yes, of course. Hebrews one fourteen. 'Bye."

From inside the house I watched Jon. He sat in the driveway for a moment. Then ever so slowly he backed the truck toward the street. Twice he stopped, turned, and looked long and hard into the bed of the truck.

Back in the kitchen, I did a little impromptu dance. The kitchen overflowed with the aroma of roast beef and gingerbread and an unmistakable sense of the glory of God. In about fifteen minutes the phone rang.

"Mom. It's Jon."

For once I didn't bombard him with questions. I just held the phone calmly and waited to see what he had to say. "Hi, Jon."

"The thing is, Mom, my truck had a flat tire and I wound up in a ditch. I'm okay though. I'm at a pay phone. Some man appeared from nowhere and together we got my truck back on the road. Listen, after we change the tire . . . I mean . . . have you eaten? I don't think I'm going to the party after all."

"I haven't eaten, and I forgot to tell you—I made gravy."

"Will you wait for me? I'm coming home."

"I'll wait."

All these years later, the sweetness of that moment is one of my finest memories.

I was putting ice in the glasses when I heard the unmistakable roar of Jon's truck. I didn't run out to meet him, except in my heart. I swallowed hard, wiped my eyes quickly on my apron and said aloud, "Oh, thank You, Lord!"

Jon came bounding in, looking remarkably like his father. "Supper sure smells good, Mom. But first I wonder if—well, the thing is that I'm probably the only boy in Georgia with a truck-load of angels. Could you—get 'em out?"

"Certainly," I said, flashing my best smile. I marched to the front door with Jon close behind, stepped onto the porch in the twilight, and took off my apron. "Thanks so much, fellows," I said, as though I dismissed angels routinely. "You can all leave now. But don't go too far." I waved for a bit.

Finally Jon and I sat down at the kitchen table with a feast before us. Jon talked, going on about the engine of his truck. I had no idea what a fuel pump was, but I leaned forward, listening intently, nodding my head, feeling a little bit like the mother of the year. We had the best conversation in heavens knew how long. "You know, Mom," Jon said over dessert, "you're pretty good company—for a mom, I mean."

Of course, that was only because I kept company with angels.

Now, almost twenty years later, as Jon fought for his life against the infection in his right hand, I prayed angels into the operating room each time he went to surgery. I even managed to thank God that Jon was left-handed.

I somehow let go of the anger and resentment that had set in two years before when he called from Dunklin, the tone of his voice telling me that something was terribly wrong. He'd graduated the program in February. The whole family flew down to be with him as he stood with the nine other men who had completed the program. Jon told us that he felt God wanted him to take an additional ten-week program called Servant Leadership Training. He was nearly through. The staff wanted him to stay on and become a counselor.

But then the phone call came. "Mom," Jon said, "I've been kicked out of camp. I have to leave immediately. I—I was taken to the emergency room with a severe infection. The doctor made a mistake and gave me a prescription for the pain. I knew better, but I got it filled and sold some and gave some away—and of course, I took some." His voice was full of the rage that I hadn't heard in nearly a year—the voice of the old Jon; nothing was his fault.

I felt as though I had turned to stone.

"You can't stay here," I made myself say. "You can go into another drug program nearby." It was one of the most difficult things I'd ever said, but I knew that men who managed to get kicked out of Dunklin often went deeper into drugs.

Jon flew back to Atlanta on the return ticket from his flight to Dunklin. I didn't meet the plane or let him stay with us, praying I was doing the right thing.

Jon found another place to live and started a rapid descent back into addiction. Surely the angels were still available. They hadn't just disappeared. Somehow I had to ignore my feelings of despair, refuse to let the fear back in and believe and pray for Jon's arm, hand and fingers, for his total restoration—for his life.

The words eased softly into my thoughts and took me to a place where fear wasn't permitted:

"Though the fig tree should not blossom
And there be no fruit on the vines,
Though the yield of the olive should fail
And the fields produce no food. . . ."

I skipped on to the promise:

"The Lord God is my strength,
And He has made my feet like hinds' feet. . . ."

I glanced down at my feet, size eight-and-a-half, in white socks and worn sneakers, and squinted, imagining that they'd turned into tiny hinds' feet, able to walk anywhere—victoriously, fearlessly.

Father, I always thought angels were just something to put on the Christmas tree. Maybe they were around in biblical days. But for most of my life, I never considered that they could be here, doing Your work—protecting, encouraging, fighting the evil one, ministering, directing. But I believe in them now, I really do, in life-and-death situations and in small events of daily life. Help me to be more aware of them. Please send some warring angels to fight for Jon's life, his arm, his hand.

PART TWO

"AND THERE BE NO
FRUIT ON THE VINES..."

6 | MY KNIGHT IN A STATION WAGON

As Gene and I were driving home from visiting Jon and Jeremy in their respective hospitals, I looked across at his face and his hands on the steering wheel. "What are you thinking?" I asked. I asked that question a lot. One of the things I first loved about Gene was that he'd open up with me—tell me his deepest thoughts and listen to mine. I could ramble on for an eternity and he'd sit and listen. He's a tremendous listener. Sometimes he cries. I like that too.

As we neared home, he reached for my hand. "I'm thinking I'm glad I can be with you and help you. That you don't have to do this alone . . ."

"Me too," I answered. We drove in silence, holding hands, and I stuck a beat-up old tape of Jim Reeves love songs—long-ago songs—in the tape player. Instantly I was falling in love with Gene all over again.

"Have I Told You Lately That I Love You?"

"Goodnight, Irene."

"My Happiness."

I'd never heard of Jim Reeves when the tape was mistakenly brought to me years ago by the Gwinnett County police. Some tapes had been stolen from my car, and I reported the theft, never expecting to see them again. A few days later, a police officer showed up at my door. "We found your tapes, Mrs. West. I think they're all here."

And indeed, they were—plus one tape that wasn't mine. As I sat in my car looking through the returned tapes, I thought God said something to me that didn't make a dab of sense: *Play that country-and-western tape by Jim Reeves.* The idea seemed ridiculous—I didn't like country-and-western music—but in case God really was speaking, I wanted to see what He was up to. The music went straight to my heart, and I started crying. The old songs sung by one of the sweetest voices I'd ever heard seemed to answer the question I couldn't get out of my mind: *Could the widower from Oklahoma I've been writing to actually be the husband I asked God to send me?* I'd never heard of God speaking through a stolen country-and-western tape before, but now He was telling me in no uncertain terms, *Yes, Yes, Yes! Gene Acuff is the husband you've been asking me to send you!*

I'd been a widow for four years, and I longed to be a wife again. I didn't really want to date—I just wanted another chance at being a wife. I'd written down something in my Bible that the great missionary Hudson Taylor had said: "God reserves the best for those who leave the choice to Him." Several months before I'd made a list of the requirements I wanted in a husband and told God I'd leave the choice to Him.

I'd thought God had whispered to my heart: *I'm sending him!*

But then I argued with myself: *Why would God do that for me? Who am I? Nobody special. And if I were really a good mother, I wouldn't be having so much trouble with Jon and Jeremy. I probably wouldn't be a good wife either.* I looked over my list of requirements again. *Would God really take me seriously?*

1. God must be first in his life. I want to be second.
2. He's well-read and loves books.

3. He's further along than I am spiritually.
4. I'd like to be a minister's wife, but I'll leave that up to You, Lord.
5. He has a deep sense of humor, so that we can laugh together.
6. He's able to communicate and have long conversations.
7. He cares about people, especially people who are hurting.
8. He will allow me to write and speak as long as You want me to, Lord.
9. He needs me.
10. There must be sparks! Romance.

I'd thought God said something like: *I'm going to answer your prayer for a husband. The answer will come very quickly—so fast it will scare you if you don't trust Me completely. The answer will come through a phone call from a reader in response to an article you've written.*

"When will I know for certain, Lord?" I'd asked.

By your birthday.

So by July 8, 1987, I should know something. In April of that year *Guideposts* magazine published an article I'd written on depression. That article evoked phone calls and letters from quite a few men going through the pain of losing their wives.

On April 8 I received a telephone call from Gene Acuff, a professor of sociology at Oklahoma State University in Stillwater. He lived on a small farm with some cattle, a grown son, and a red dog. He was also a minister. Soon we were having conversations three or four times a week. And then the professor/minister/farmer and I were writing to each other almost every day. Our letters weren't love letters exactly, but there was always something between the lines, and I easily understood the unwritten messages.

Sometimes Gene enclosed a blank sheet of paper with his letters. "What's with the blank paper?" I finally wrote.

His answer came immediately: "Things I want to say to you that you aren't yet ready to hear."

Gene planned to come to Atlanta to see me. He's always said that I invited him, but I didn't. "What do you want to see?" I asked. "Where do you want to go?"

"I just want to see you. No parties, no big plans. I want to walk with you, talk and laugh. I want to sit on a porch swing with you, and I'd like to go somewhere under a tin roof and listen to the rain with you." I was smiling as I held the phone. I smiled a lot when we talked. We were talking six to eight hours a week. My mother said I had a certain light back in my eyes again.

Of course I told myself this wasn't serious. We really didn't know each other. We'd just get acquainted, have some good conversation and good food, and relate our experiences of grief and loss. Gene's wife of twenty-five years had died that February. His loss was much too recent for us to be serious. I had no way of knowing then that when Gene read my article on depression, God spoke to him: *Check your wife's Bible. If she has the same Scriptures underlined that Marion used in the article, phone Marion right away.* She did, and he did. Although neither of us understood it or could explain it, he said God told him, *She will be your new wife.*

On my fifty-first birthday I went to get the mail as soon as I saw the mailman put it in the box. I knew a letter from Gene would arrive. He'd already sent me a dozen red roses; he'd said something about photographs. So far, the only picture of him I had was a very small family portrait taken several years before. I wanted some new pictures, but I wouldn't ask for them.

There were two letters that morning, one so thick I knew it had the promised pictures. I was late for an appointment and it was terribly hot, so I sat in my car with the air-conditioning going full blast and read the letters. Just as I opened the thick envelope, God seemed to tell me to play the Jim Reeves tape. When I heard, "Evening shadows make me blue/when each weary day is through/how I long to be with you,/my happiness," tears blurred my vision. I whispered out loud over my pounding heart, "God, you can't possibly be speaking to me through a stolen tape!" I held the photographs in my hand and looked intently at Gene's smiling face and then at his dog. The dog was smiling too! His expression clearly said, *He's pretty wonderful!*

"If I could take you out on your birthday," Gene had written, "I'd pick you up in my old '41 Chevy, and we'd go to a 1950s movie and eat popcorn and drink Cokes from the little bottles, and, of course, we'd eat Milk Duds at the movies."

"Milk Duds!" I shouted over the music, my heart melting like hot butter. No one knew about my passion for Milk Duds. How could Gene Acuff know? Jim Reeves was singing, "Have I Told You Lately That I Love You?" and I was humming along and trying not to cry on the photos—as I drove to my appointment an hour late.

That night Gene phoned, and as we were about to hang up he said for the first time, "I love you, Marion."

"Thank you. 'Bye," I answered curtly and hung up.

He said the same thing two nights later, and I gave the same response. Only this time I hid under my pillow after hanging up and said, "Oh, God, I don't know how to handle this."

The third time he told me that he loved me there was a long

silence. Then Gene asked, "Are you going to say what I want you to say?"

I took a deep breath. I felt as though I were a child about to jump off a high diving board. "I love you, Professor Acuff. I really do love you." I had often wondered what his response would be if I ever said those words.

His response wasn't to me at all: "Thank You, Lord. Oh, thank You. Praise You, Lord Jesus."

We agreed that Gene would come to Georgia at the end of the month. We'd meet at the Stone Mountain Inn, not far from my house. The waiting was almost unbearable. I lost twelve pounds and was hardly sleeping.

At noon on July 27, my phone rang, and the voice I knew so well said, "Hello."

"Where are you?" I asked.

"Stone Mountain Inn."

"I'll be there in ten minutes."

When I pulled into the driveway of the inn, someone honked at me. Looking into the rearview mirror, I recognized Gene in his station wagon. I didn't know what to do. I thought about sitting in the car and letting him come over. But it was just like in the movies: I left my car with the engine running in the middle of the driveway, the door open. As we rushed toward each other, my sunglasses dropped on the pavement and one shoe fell off. Just as we embraced, I remembered the advice I'd given my girls when they were growing up: "No public displays of affection *ever*." But right there in the middle of the parking lot, in broad daylight, with people all around us, we kissed. I lost count of the times.

I'd planned a picnic for just the two of us the next day at my cousin's house, a one-hundred-and-fifty-year-old renovated farmhouse in northeast Georgia. I thought Gene would feel at home there: There were even cattle and three swings and a tin roof. Sitting on an antique loveseat in front of a stone fireplace, Gene started to ask me to marry him in December.

Suddenly I felt a sharp pain—an old ulcer was acting up. All the stress had caught up with me. Gene and I were deeply in love, and we knew God had brought us together. But he had to return to Oklahoma to teach, and I didn't see how I could pull up stakes and go with him. Jeremy and Jon, almost twenty, still lived with me. I was afraid to leave them alone for even a night, certain they would break some of my rules. Julie, her husband, and their two daughters lived nearby, as did Jennifer and her husband, who were expecting their first child. My mother lived less than an hour and a half away. All my dearest friends were in Georgia. And I was booked to speak for the next six months.

Gene had to move to the far end of the loveseat. Every time he came close, my stomach pains intensified. He held onto my foot—I found I could tolerate foot-holding pretty well—and asked me to marry him. I said yes. We talked about maintaining two separate residences and commuting often. Two days later, in exactly two minutes, we selected an engagement ring.

Then it was Sunday. Our week was over. Gene left crying, and I went to my room crying and fell across my bed begging God to "do something." He somehow knocked me out. Totally. When Gene, en route back to Oklahoma in his station wagon, phoned my house, neither Jon nor Jeremy could awaken me. When I did wake up four hours later and they told me he had called, I somehow knew I had to clear my calendar. I started phoning people, asking to be relieved of speaking engagements.

In eleven years of speaking, I'd never done such a thing, except when Jerry had had brain surgery.

Gene later called from Tennessee and asked, "Could you marry me a week from Wednesday?" Rather than December, he meant. I checked my calendar and said yes and wrote, "Marry Gene on August 12."

As it turned out, the wedding—a very small ceremony—was moved to August 14, at seven in the evening. Gene and I honeymooned at my cousin's restored farmhouse. We sort of identified with it: Gene and I understood something about restoration. The night before we left the farm, God sent the rain we'd so often talked and written about. As we listened to it hit the tin roof, Gene said quietly. "Your formula works, Marion."

"What formula?"

"The restoration formula you wrote about in your book."

Oh yes! It did work. I could remember the formula from *The Nevertheless Principle* almost word for word. While I watched my husband Jerry slowly dying, I carefully examined the restoration formula God had given me:

"No matter what's taken away from you, if you keep your eyes on Jesus and praise Him, He will restore it to you. You will be joyful to the exact same degree you have hurt. What you have lost will be replaced . . . joy for mourning . . . beauty for ashes. . . ."

On August 22, 1987, Gene and I headed for the Atlanta airport and a new life together. Gene never asked me to leave my sons. He was content to have a marriage in which we commuted for a while. But God told me clearly, *Quit hovering over your sons. You are trying to be their god. Let Me be God to them.*

I'd often said after Jerry was gone that if God ever asked me to simply walk out on everything, I would. I had assumed that it would be for the missions—Africa, not Stillwater, Oklahoma! But God had recently given me an old Scripture with a marvelous life-changing message: "The Lord is my shepherd; I shall not want . . . He leadeth me beside the still waters. He restoreth my soul. . . ."

Lord Jesus, You've done some pretty awesome things for me. You sent me a husband. You told me You would and then You did it, even though I doubted. I don't want to doubt about Jon's life and arm and hand now. I want to believe with all my heart. Will You help me to believe for his healing? Will You enable me not to look at circumstances, but to look only to You, just You? I desperately need to fasten my hope on You.

GOOD GRIEF | 7

DURING THOSE FIRST WEEKS in Stillwater, Oklahoma, I'd awaken early and tiptoe alone to the patio to watch the sun rise over the barn. Its sudden explosion of radiant light reminded me of our sudden love. The dark, lonely days were really over!

On those brilliant mornings my prayer was always the same. "God, I don't know how to thank You. I didn't think there would ever be anyone, and You sent Gene to me. Thank You. Oh, thank You."

But I'd overlooked the obvious in my fairy-tale romance. I was moving into the home where Gene and his former wife, Phyllis, had lived, dreamed, loved and raised their children. Phyllis had been gone only a short time when Gene first phoned me; we had gotten married just six months after her sudden death. "I've worked through the grief," Gene had assured me.

When I first stepped inside Gene's country home with him and met some of his children and grandchildren, they smiled, hugged me, and said welcoming things, but I could see the grief in their eyes.

It made me wonder, *Is Gene grieving too?* My luggage, piled on the floor, suddenly looked out of place—and I felt out of place too. I didn't want to deal with grief again. My own had nearly destroyed me.

Shortly after arriving, I found a place of solace in my new home. When Gene looked sad or attempted to remember Phyllis,

I learned to retreat to a beautiful pink bathroom with wallpaper that reminded me of some back in the home I'd left in Georgia. Fixing my eyes on the sweetly familiar paper, I'd reason: *Maybe I can live in this lovely bathroom. It's roomy but cozy. I just can't go out there and battle grief again.*

We'd been married about two months when I decided to make Gene a cup of hot spiced tea. As I handed him the cup, a look of sadness crossed his face. He took the steaming tea to the kitchen table and set it down. We both stared at it mutely, and I knew: Phyllis had made that same kind of tea. I didn't want him to tell me about it. And he didn't.

Gene suggested we go for a walk. Each day we walked around the pasture with Elmo, Gene's golden retriever, and Bobby, a stray kitten we'd taken in. The sun was low and the air nippy, so we'd bundled up, held hands, and walked fast. Gene said, "You walk faster than Phyllis." Then he was silent.

I thought, *Only a few months ago he was walking in this same pasture with another wife.* I knew he needed to talk, but I was afraid that he would and I'd be drawn back into grief again.

Then, without warning, a silent voice spoke clearly to my heart: *Marion, you need to grieve for Phyllis.* I wasn't praying or asking God anything, and the strange message so startled me that I slowed my pace.

"What's wrong?" Gene asked, slowing down beside me.

"Nothing," I said, quickening my step. I wanted to think about the message more carefully before sharing it with Gene.

I waited a week before telling Gene I believed God wanted me to grieve with him for Phyllis. A look that was difficult to explain crossed his face: pain, laced with enormous relief and gratitude.

I had no idea how to grieve for someone I'd never known,

someone I didn't even want to think about, but I wanted to be willing to follow God's instructions.

The next day I was searching for some Scotch tape and discovered a cabinet where Phyllis had kept all of her gift-wrapping supplies, right next to the pink bathroom. It was crammed full of fancy paper, ribbons, new greeting cards, tape, gift lists, mailing supplies. I adored the cabinet. Most of my cabinets and closets back in Georgia were jumbled, just like this one. There were days, while Gene lectured at Oklahoma State University, that I went to the "clutter cabinet" not really needing anything; I just opened it and stood there, inhaling the lovely feeling it always gave me.

As I searched through the cabinet, I realized what a giver Phyllis had been. There were lists of things she planned to buy for people. As I continued to explore the clutter cabinet, I began to know Phyllis.

Gene encouraged me to open drawers, look at scrapbooks, do anything necessary to make myself feel at home. I admired the many lovely antiques and touched some of them gently. I picked up some of Phyllis's books—we liked the same books. I dusted her grand piano and antique organ carefully, almost reverently.

While looking through a drawer one day, I found a lipstick. I held it tightly in my hand, feeling I had no right even to touch it, but unable to put it down. Finally I pulled the top off. It wasn't some harsh red or bright purple, but a lovely shade of coral. I leaned toward the mirror and applied some of the lipstick, and a thought surfaced, a memory from high school: *Only best friends use each other's lipstick.* I slipped the tube of lipstick into my skirt pocket and carried it wherever I went for weeks. Somehow it gave me courage.

The first snow of the season came unexpectedly early. "Gene, let's go out in the snow!" I begged.

A startled look came over him. "Phyllis used to beg me to play in the snow with her," he said. "She loved it. I never wanted to. I had to work outside in the snow with the cattle, and so snow never meant fun to me."

All the time he spoke, he was putting on his boots, gloves, warm coat and bright-orange hat. Elmo joined us outside. The fresh snow crunched beneath our feet. Gene stopped suddenly, looking down the road in front of the house as though he saw something in the distance. "The last time it snowed, nine months ago, Phyllis wanted me to walk down that road with her. She begged me to. I didn't. I remember so clearly that she and Elmo walked without me . . . I watched from inside."

I squinted and looked down the white country road, and I could almost see them.

Back inside, we were getting out of our coats and boots when I looked at Gene and recognized his grief. I almost gasped. With great difficulty, barely above a whisper, he managed to say, "I keep thinking she's coming back."

Holding his face in my cold hands, I silently asked God what to do. I was shocked at what came out of my mouth. Gently but firmly, looking Gene right in the eyes, I said, "It's over, Gene. She's never coming back. Phyllis is gone. *Really* gone. She's okay now, but she's never coming back."

Gene began to cry. We held on to each other, and I cried too. He cried for a long time. When the tears were over, he said, "You two would have liked each other."

But the struggle was far from over. The following Fourth of July was one of Gene's most difficult days. Phyllis had loved the Fourth, and she and Gene had always had friends and family over, with lots of food and fireworks. Gene and I chose to spend the Fourth alone, almost anticipating the grief the day would bring. We were both quiet, seeming to realize that no words would help—this day could only be endured. Gene sat in his favorite recliner, sometimes speaking in broken sentences and sometimes remembering quietly. I sat close by on the sofa. We hurt together. Instead of driving us apart, the shared grief was bringing us even closer together.

One day the following month, Gene and I went swimming in his daughter Jo Shelley's pool (she lived about three miles from our farm). Now that I "knew" Phyllis I could see her radiant smile in Shelley's expression. Gene didn't really enjoy swimming, but he hadn't made the time to swim with Phyllis, so now he wanted to swim with me. We were hanging onto a raft, still discussing grief, when Gene asked, "Why does it have to hurt so much, Marion?"

I felt God guiding me to an explanation, and I said, "Gene, this might be the answer: Grief is to healing what labor is to delivering a baby. To prevent it or even slow it down would be unnatural, disastrous. Grief is really our unsuspected friend who introduces us to healing."

After that, we talked more openly about grief. I told Gene about the time I was flying to speak to a group. Jerry had been dead two years, and I hadn't hurt for several days. I had assumed that my grieving process was finally over. I felt confident, secure. Then a man in the seat next to me opened a pack of peanuts and rolled them around in his hand for a moment before slowly popping them one at a time into his mouth. Jerry had eaten peanuts exactly like that. I was pulled back into fresh, smothering grief.

"Did you ever think you were losing your mind?" Gene asked suddenly.

"Oh yes! That's a real part of grief. It will pass, but you don't know that while it's smothering you."

When we were about to celebrate our first wedding anniversary, I went to the clutter cabinet for ribbon for Gene's gift. A few bright ribbons fluttered to the floor, along with a card I'd never seen. I picked up the card. On the front were two smiling bears, one holding a bridal bouquet. It read, "Congratulations. God has given you the best—each other. 'Delight thyself also in the Lord; and he shall give thee the desires of thine heart'" (Psalm 37:4). Phyllis had bought the card for someone else, but for a few precious, crazy moments, the card was from Phyllis to me.

That evening I pulled out the card and told Gene what happened, and he smiled. There was no surface grief. At last Gene had worked his way through it—to joy.

Father, thank You for reminding me of good times, answered prayers, great joy—loving Gene and our being in Oklahoma together. Thank You for teaching us that grief is a very necessary emotion, and for giving us the grace to walk through it, so healing can begin. The hurt I feel for Jeremy and Jon is a lot like grief, Father. Help me find the healing on the other side—for all of us.

THE TOWN I | 8
PLANNED TO HATE |

I LOVED LIVING IN OKLAHOMA with Gene out on his farm, six miles from town, but I still had concerns about my nineteen-year-old sons back in Georgia. When I called home, people I didn't even know answered the telephone at my house! Jon and Jeremy always had some excuse that I was suppose to believe. Deep in my heart, I knew they weren't living right. I prayed for them, and so did Gene and the people at the church we went to. For the most part I didn't spend all day with anxious thoughts as I had when I was living with them. I loved my storybook life until one day, Gene said, beaming, "Guess what? I took a position as interim minister at Perry First Christian Church. It's about forty minutes from here. I told them we'd come right away—this Sunday."

Our first argument ensued. "You what?" I bellowed. "Without talking it over with me? I don't want to go to Perry. We're supposed to be moving back to Georgia. You're officially retired from the university now. I'm not going to Perry."

Gene looked stunned. I knew my attitude was rotten.

"I should have talked with you, honey," Gene said sincerely. "I'd really like to preach again." He had been a minister for twenty-eight years in a nearby country church in addition to teaching at OSU.

"Okay, okay!" I said loudly, "I'll commute with you to Perry and I'll be a dutiful minister's wife, but you should know I plan to detest every minute of it."

His face lit up just as though I'd been cooperative. "Thanks. As soon as the farm sells, we'll be on our way to Georgia to live, just as we planned." The farm had been for sale for more than a year, and it appeared it would never sell.

In church the following Sunday in Perry, I found a seat near the front, determined to sit alone. Just as the service got under way, a smiling older couple got up from their seats and came to sit with me as though we were old friends. When Gene started to pray, the woman reached over and held my hand. No one else was holding hands. For such a petite lady, she certainly had a powerful grip. She offered to share her hymnal with me, but I pretended not to notice.

Monday we drove back to Perry in silence. At the church I couldn't bring myself to go inside while Gene worked in his office. "I'm going to town," I announced with a flair of independence.

Gene handed me the car keys. "Have a good time."

Feeling like a blob, I drove the three short blocks to "town." I parked and got out of the car, slamming the door harder than necessary. I felt ridiculous—I couldn't even think of anything to buy. Hoping I looked confident, I started across the street against the light. A red truck slammed on its brakes. *Oh, Lord, if he hollers at me, I'm going to cry.* A smiling man leaned out of the truck, motioned me on and waved. "Thanks," I called out.

"You bet," he said.

Oh my goodness. I hadn't expected a town square. I stood there gazing helplessly as sweet memories of my own hometown square in Elberton, Georgia, poured through my emotions like a balm. There's something marvelously secure about a town with a square. It's almost as though the town has a real heart and the ability to care. A gazebo, bandstand, manicured lawn, giant shade trees, picnic tables, a cannon, little paths—everything in this tiny town of about five thousand. Almost reverently, I sat on a bench and looked around.

Then I caught myself. *So what if the town has a square? I'm still not going to like it.*

I strolled around the square despite the heat and entered Foster's corner drugstore. I sat on a stool at a real old-fashioned soda fountain. The hand-lettered sign said, CHERRY COKES, and I hadn't had one since I was a teenager. I ordered one and asked the smiling woman behind the counter, "Do you make chocolate sodas too?"

"You bet. Best in town. You'll have to come back."

Back outside, a bright yellow sign beckoned to me: THE PERRY DAILY JOURNAL. I was surprised that a town so small would have a daily paper. I went in to buy a paper to read about the town that I planned to hate.

The minute I stepped inside the glass door, a long-forgotten childhood memory surfaced. Even as a youngster, I knew I wanted to be a writer—and oh, how I longed to meet a real, live writer, any kind of writer! Of course, there weren't any in Elberton, except for a veteran reporter who had his own column at our newspaper, *The Elberton Star*. I thought up reasons to go to the *Star* office to buy things from Mr. Herbert Wilcox. Pencils, poster board, even newspapers. He'd smile over his small, round glasses when I entered, get up from his ancient typewriter, and ask, "May I help you, young lady?"

As I stood in the office of *The Perry Daily Journal*, which looked amazingly like the *Star* office back in the fifties, a distinguished white-haired gentleman rose promptly from his outdated typewriter. "May I help you?" he asked. I felt thirteen rather than fifty-three.

When I found my voice, I couldn't blurt out, "Could you just talk to me for a while?" Instead, I said casually, "I'd like to buy a paper." Even so, I spilled my change on the counter.

I left the office reading the paper. The man must have been Milo Watson, editor and publisher of *The Perry Daily Journal* for forty-two years. In large, bold letters I read: SAY SOMETHING GOOD ABOUT PERRY TODAY! I stopped smiling abruptly. This was the town I'd planned to hate!

Later that week Gene asked me to go with him to visit a church member in the hospital. After parking the car we observed an unusual truck parked in the lot. The back was crammed full of iron pipes and junk, and standing on top of it all was a goat! I hesitated. "That goat's fine, Marion," Gene called. He knew my passion for rescuing stray animals.

"Then why has someone tied him to that old iron pipe?" I asked, running to the hospital ahead of Gene to find the owner and ask questions. By the time Gene found me I was talking to a tired-looking man in overalls.

"Yes, that's my goat. Or rather, my wife's. She thinks more of that goat than she does me. Crazy goat hides in the back of my truck and hitches a ride to town. Then he sneaks off and heads for the square." I nodded. The story made sense. "Today some friends of mine noticed him—out in the middle of the street again, stopping traffic. They chased him down and tied him in the back of my truck. Everyone knows my truck and my goat. We're heading home now."

I smiled a lot that day.

A couple of days later, I decided to write a note to a church member visiting from Albuquerque. I couldn't find a dictionary at the church, so I dialed the post office. "Do you know how to spell *Albuquerque?*" I asked. Slowly, patiently, the man spelled it for me.

"Thanks," I said.

"You bet."

People in Oklahoma use that expression a lot. I like it. Short and to the point. No frills.

After we'd been in Perry for a few weeks, Gene came up with an idea. "Marion, tonight in church I want you to share with the people how you planned to hate this town."

"Oh, Gene, I can't. I won't."

"Of course you can. We've been studying how God can change attitudes——"

"Well, mine isn't completely changed," I snapped.

Gene went ahead and announced my talk in the morning service. That evening I stood looking into gentle, open faces, the kind that simply expect you to speak the complete truth.

"I . . . I . . . planned to hate this town," I said. They never flinched or dropped their eyes. "I didn't know Perry would have a square and sidewalks and chimes that ring at noon. I didn't know that paying bills was a social event—that is, you don't mail them, but rather walk around the square, visiting as you leave your checks. People care here—so much that Mrs. Lynch, who's a hundred and two, can live alone. Everyone checks on her. The waitresses even know my favorite kind of pie, and before I ask, they tell me that they have it. People sit on their porches and wave to you . . ."

I got a lot of hugs afterward. How, I wondered, could I ever have planned to hate this town?

That night before I went to sleep, I confessed, *Dear Lord, sometimes it's a glorious thing to be wrong. Thank You for bringing us to Perry. And,* I added, *for changing my attitude.*

I was beginning to feel as though we lived snugly inside a Norman Rockwell painting when in December, the farm sold. I'd almost forgotten it was for sale. "Well, now we can move to Georgia, just like we planned," Gene said. I nodded.

But after we packed up all the furniture and shipped it to my home in Georgia, I found myself saying, "Gene, we can't leave until the church gets a minister."

He stared at me. "But we planned to leave as soon as the farm sold."

"Let's move into the parsonage. We can borrow some furniture."

He smiled slightly. "That could be a long time. Are you sure?"

"You bet."

I laughed to myself. Nothing had gone as I'd hoped or even prayed. Nevertheless, here I was in Perry, Oklahoma, totally happy and walking on those amazing hinds' feet once more.

Father, thank You for the memories, for showing me how wrong I often am. I don't know nearly as much as I sometimes think I do. What patience You have with me! I want to always trust You— whether things make one dab of sense or not.

BACK TO GEORGIA | 9

THE NINE MONTHS Gene and I lived in the parsonage in Perry surprised me in many ways. There was no furniture in the parsonage, but members of the congregation donated things, and because Gene told them, "Marion and I sleep on a king-sized bed," they determined to rig one up for us.

A small cot was wired to a regular-sized bed. Of course it was about two inches lower than the bed, but it had been put together with so much love and enthusiasm that we learned to sleep in it. Often we went to sleep laughing hysterically. I was content, even happy, in Perry.

A new minister arrived in the early spring. We said our good-byes to the church and congregation we'd grown to love and headed for Georgia early one morning as the sun was coming up. We were driving in Gene's beloved station wagon, and we were so packed into it that I could hardly move. My feet were on boxes and I held stuff in my lap. I couldn't even get out of the car unless Gene got out and came around and helped me crawl out. Nevertheless, as we pulled out of the parsonage driveway, I asked, "Will you drive once around the square?"

"What for?" Gene asked, carefully folding his collection of maps.

"Well, because that's the way you say good-bye to a town you really love. Just do it, will you?"

So he drove slowly around the lovely square and I looked at

the stores, the trees, the gazebo, and tried to lock the picture in my mind. We stopped at a red light, the only people awake, and I took one last, fond look at the town I'd planned to hate.

I came to admire pioneer women tremendously as we drove the thousand miles to Georgia. *How did they ever do this in a wagon?*

Finally—finally—we were driving down the street that would lead us to my home on Stephens Street in Lilburn, Georgia, the house where Jon and Jeremy still lived.

Sweetly familiar things seemed to call out to me. One was the wonderful white picket fence around an old southern home that I adored. "What are you staring at?" Gene asked wearily.

"That fence. Did I ever tell you about how it ministered to me?"

"Did what?" He turned his eyes toward me. I didn't answer. "Tell me," he urged. "Go on."

"It was after Jerry died and things seemed overwhelming. I was angry and decided that life wasn't fair. I hated being alone. By my third year of widowhood, my face had become a stiff mask. *Oh, Lord, please don't let me be bitter*, I prayed often.

"I'd always admired that house. It's well over a hundred years old. Don't you just love the front porch?

"Well, a few years ago the house sat way back from a quiet road. Then Gwinnett County became the fastest-growing county in the United States. The road was widened and traffic lights went up and the town took on all the characteristics of a city. The house had hardly any front yard. Still, the dirt yard was swept clean. Flowers grew from ground that looked too hard to produce anything. The old rocking chairs on the porch rocked slightly in the breeze.

"I began to notice a small aproned woman raking, sweeping,

working with the flowers, cutting the grass out back. She even picked up the litter thrown from the cars that whizzed by.

"One day, driving down this very road, I noticed a new fence being built around that house. Each time I passed the house, I watched the progress of the fence. It went up quickly. The elderly carpenter painted it snow-white and put in an old-fashioned swinging gate. He added an overhead rose trellis and a gazebo. Then I noticed that he was painting the house to match the fence! I slowed down and crept by the house, fascinated by the beauty. Cars behind me honked.

"A few days later I pulled off the road, parked and stared long and hard at the marvelous fence. It was as if I'd been drawn there for some reason. The carpenter had done a magnificent job. I actually blinked away tears because it was so beautiful. I started my car to leave, but I couldn't. I cut the engine off, got out, and walked over and touched the fence. It still smelled of fresh paint. I heard the woman trying to crank a lawn mower out back.

"'Hi,' I called out, waving to her.

"Do you know what she did? Stood up straight and wiped her hands on her apron. I had no idea what to say or do.

"'I—I—came to see—your fence,' I managed. 'It's so beautiful.' I didn't tell her that I was near tears, desperately lonely, and in love with her fence.

"She smiled. 'Come on and let's sit on the front porch, and I'll tell you about the fence.'

"I remember I swallowed hard to keep from bawling. It was as though she were expecting me. We walked up the back steps and friendly cats followed. She opened the screen door for me. It squeaked like the long-ago, almost forgotten screen door from my childhood. I was nearly fifty years old, but somehow I felt like a child again. The kitchen was strewn with the remains of a fresh garden-vegetable supper. She didn't apologize for the disorder. We walked over worn green linoleum, down a wide hall with wooden floors, and out to the front porch.

"She told me to have a rocker, and I was suddenly overjoyed that I was on that porch with the marvelous white picket fence surrounding me. Cars whizzed by, but I felt protected, secure, at least for now. We rocked, talked, and drank sweet iced tea.

"'The fence isn't for me,' she explained matter-of-factly. 'I live here alone. But since so many people come by here every day now, I thought they would enjoy seeing something real pretty. Is anything prettier than a white picket fence?'

"'Oh no—nothing,'" I told her with absolute assurance.

"She went on telling me that people look at her fence, wave to her, and that a few like me even stop and come to sit on the porch with her.

"I asked her if she minded when the road was widened and all the newcomers moved in.

"She said that change is an important part of life and the making of character. 'Hon,' she said, 'when things happen that you don't like, you only have two choices.' I stopped rocking and leaned forward.

"'You get bitter or you get better.'"

Gene gave me a quick smile and looked back at the road.

"When I left she called out to me, 'Come back anytime. And leave the gate open. It looks more friendly.'"

"Deep inside me something unmistakable happened. In my mind I saw a hard, cold brick wall around my troubled, angry heart. I saw it crumbling. And in its place, this neat little white picket fence was being built by the Master Carpenter. I decided to leave the gate open for whatever or whomever God might bring my way. A year later, you and I were married."

Gene reached over and took my hand.

"Hey, watch where you're going, Gene," I said. "This is our turn—Stephens Street."

He slowed down and put on the right-turn blinker. I was back home—back to Jon and Jeremy. I had no idea what to expect. Each time we'd come home to visit, there'd been signs of partying—plus dishes in the sink and unmade beds. Jeremy always had the grass cut, though.

"I want to meet the lady who gave you that advice," Gene said quietly, as we pulled into the driveway.

———————————

My Father, You can use anything, any situation, to teach me. If I hadn't been hurting, I would never have stopped to touch that fence and I wouldn't have learned something important about You. Even when the carpenter started to build the fence, You knew that one day I'd drive down Five Forks Trickum Road and that only a white picket fence could get my attention. Help me to trust that even now You're planning something better for Jeremy and Jon than I can imagine.

PART THREE

"THOUGH THE YIELD OF THE OLIVE SHOULD FAIL . . ."

10 | MULBERRY GROVE

GENE AND I COULDN'T FIGURE OUT what to do when Jeremy and Jon were discharged from the hospital. We couldn't care for them ourselves. We had to believe God would show us a way where there seemed to be no way. He had done it before.

Amazingly, neither Jeremy nor Jon complained much in their respective hospitals. Jeremy's room felt subdued, quiet. He didn't speak unless we asked him something. He managed to eat good meals—the prescriptions for his bipolar disorder seemed to keep him hungry. One hundred and fifty was his normal, skinny weight at a little over six feet. Now it was hovering around two hundred.

Jon, on the other hand, was losing weight. One day when he put on his denim shorts to walk in the halls pushing his IV pole, they actually fell down. I was walking with him, so I caught them around his knees and slid them back up while he laughed and passersby smiled or tried not to. His usual weight at six feet two inches was something over two hundred. I suppose some of the drugs he'd been using had taken away his appetite. He seemed to always be smiling, joking, managing to be grateful that he was left-handed, since it was his right hand that he was in danger of losing.

When he was moved out of ICU into a private room, there was almost a party atmosphere. Laughing people came and went and there were balloons and other gifts from friends—candy, a steak dinner one night, golf magazines, new flip-flops. His laughter often tumbled down the halls, and I heard it as I approached his room.

The routine of daily hospital visits and waiting for the results of Jon's many surgeries was exhausting. Mostly, I was numb. But there was an upside to the whole mess: Each of my sons was restrained and well cared for and not out doing Lord knows what. It would come to an end soon, but at night when I fell asleep, I never had to wonder: *Where is Jon? Where is Jeremy? Are they both alive?*

Jon's hand took a turn for the worse, and we reinforced our prayers. Jon understood clearly that he might lose his hand. When Gene and I walked into his room one day before surgery, he was standing in the middle of the floor talking on the phone. He was laughing and crying, his right hand held in the air with the huge bandage that looked like a white boxing glove. "Hey, buddy, great to hear your voice. Listen, I need all the brothers there to pray for me. And—you were right to kick me out of camp. I deserved it. I want to thank you for being tough with me. I love you, too, brother."

Then he shut his eyes, held the phone in the crook of his neck, and raised both hands high in the air in praise.

Gene and I bowed our heads and silently prayed. From what I'd heard of the conversation, I knew Jon had called Dunklin and managed to get Dave Pittman on the phone. No one ever got Dave on the phone without many calls. He was the one who had said, "Come on down here, Jon. We have a bed for you." Dave, also a twin, had once been a drug addict, like everyone on staff at Dunklin. Now he was married and the father of three beautiful girls. He and his wife lived at the camp. Dave played hardball with the addicted men—he had to. As painful as Jon's dismissal from Dunklin had been, I knew Dave had been absolutely right, and I thanked God for his toughness.

"Amen! Amen! Thank You, Jesus," Jon was saying through his tears. When Jon talked about Jesus or special Scriptures now, he'd start to cry. He insisted his relationship with Jesus was intact, even though he was walking in disobedience. He would start practically preaching about grace if anyone said anything to him about loving God, being a born-again Christian, and living as a druggie. Mostly, I didn't discuss it with him.

His sister Julie had pointed out, "Mother, how do we know that our continual fear and worry isn't a worse sin than being addicted to drugs or whatever?"

Julie wasn't usually vocal, but she could come up with pointed, painful questions that I often couldn't answer. And she was the most nonjudgmental person I'd ever known, always expecting the best from everyone.

She'd been a junior mom to me when Jon and Jeremy were born, when she was almost eight and Jennifer almost six. By the time she was ten, she could have raised Jon and Jeremy and Jen too. She never complained when I asked her to help me with them—and I asked a lot.

As a grown woman and the mother of three herself, Julie confessed something to me one day. We were talking on the phone and she put laughter in her voice to take the edge off the words. "Mama, do you know I thought it was my sole purpose in life to make you happy? I tried *so* hard. Everyday I prayed, 'God let me make her happier today. Let me keep her from screaming at the boys.'"

Marion, say something. Keep this conversation going. This has been pent up in your daughter for decades.

"I—I—didn't know, Julie. You never complained or . . ."

"I could see you were trying as hard as you could. It shouldn't have been so hard. I wanted to help you, to make life easier . . ."

"And you did. Oh, how you did. But I should have stopped and realized that you were just a child—a child who never asked for anything or complained . . ."

"Well, we got them raised, didn't we, Mama?"

"Yes, and I owe you, Julie. I'll never be able to repay you for all the strolls you took them on, diapers you changed, games you played with them, dangers you kept them from. . . ."

"It's still hard though, Mother. You are still so involved in their lives. I keep thinking that surely things will turn around for them, for you. . . ."

And she was there at the hospital nearly every day for both of them, always laughing, smiling, encouraging them, recalling a funny or happy memory from their childhood.

Oh, God, I wish I hadn't expected so much of Julie. If only I could mother them all over again.

Jeremy was scheduled to be released from the hospital first. The social worker at the hospital told me confidentially, "Jeremy can go back to his house. We can arrange for a hospital bed to be brought in and have one hot meal a day delivered there. Someone will check on him several times a week. I've already done the paperwork, and he's agreed to go. He leaves tomorrow afternoon." She was young, overworked and relieved to have one fewer patient. She wanted me to smile and say thank you and get out of her way.

"You can't do that," I said. "That house is filthy and mildewed. I'm not even sure if the power is on or there's any water. There's no room for a hospital bed. The rooms are cluttered and full of garbage. Besides, he's still wearing a catheter, and he's depressed and has to have all his medicine. Living isn't high on his list of priorities now. That house has horrible memories. . . ."

"Jeremy is able to make decisions for himself," she replied. "He's thirty-five, and the paperwork is done. The hospital bed is being delivered. Jeremy has adjusted. Now you need to."

Anger roared through me. I asked God to calm me down somehow. I didn't want to start screaming in the hospital hallway.

I spoke quietly, but the rage was just beneath the surface. "Jeremy is not going to that place. He has to be cared for, and he cannot come to our house. We had him with us for three months and he lied to us and huffed aerosol cleaner. Because he can't come home with us doesn't mean we don't love him. There has to be another way. I'll be glad to work with you and I'll do the leg-work, but don't tell me again that he's going to that—place. . . ."

She turned and walked away briskly with her papers and charts, her shoulder-length hair swinging angrily. "It's okay," Jeremy told us as we stood at the foot of his bed. "I want to go home." And he meant it. He wouldn't ask for anything.

Then an idea came to Julie and Gene. I have no doubt that it was from God. "Mulberry Grove," they both told me. My mother had been a patient at Mulberry Grove before she died; Jeremy's paternal grandparents, Ada and Robert West, had also lived there for a short time. It was a lovely assisted-living place, with huge pecan trees out front, a circular driveway and a front porch with rocking chairs. But I'd never known of anyone as young as Jeremy being admitted to an assisted-living facility.

It was Saturday; crises always happen on weekends. I got Patty Moody's home number—she's the owner of Mulberry Grove— and dialed. I got her answering machine. "Patty, it's Marion. Could you possibly take another one of us? It's Jeremy—you remember, one of my twins. He visited his grandparents there. He has broken bones and needs a place to stay for a few months."

While visions of an ambulance taking Jeremy back to his house invaded my mind, I tried to pray. *God, make a place for him. Show us a plan.*

The phone rang. Patty laughed a bit, and in her wonderful, carefree-sounding voice, said, "Hi, Marion. We'd love to have Jeremy, but he'll have to be evaluated by our nurse first. We've taken folks with broken bones before for short-term stays. I think it'll work."

Jeremy wasn't thrilled about going to Mulberry Grove—to an "old folks home"—and he was even less thrilled to learn that he'd have to pay for it out of the money he'd been left recently by his Grandfather West. He wanted to come home with us and thought if he looked unhappy enough, we'd change our minds. But even if we'd wanted to give him another chance to live with us, we couldn't have met his medical needs—we couldn't even lift him from his bed.

Oh, Father, fear was breathing down my neck and I almost gave into it when I couldn't see a way to find a place for Jeremy. Your strength is amazing. I so want to trust You when things don't seem to be working out. Thank You for Mulberry Grove, for a room for Jeremy.

11 | ROSEMARY'S GIFT

IT WAS NEARLY CHRISTMAS. Julie and I were standing in the large circular room just inside the front door of Mulberry Grove. So far Jeremy hadn't taken to life there; he stayed sulking in his room. I spent as much time with him as I could.

"Mother," Julie said, "I think you're doing too much for Jeremy. He's getting good care, good food, friendship. You run back and forth to Mulberry Grove as though he were a child." Julie smiled. Her eyes said, *I love you. I care that things are so hard.*

Julie was right. And now, as I looked into her eyes, I knew why. Emotionally, I was back where I was when Jeremy was nine months old and nearly dying, so near Christmas. The pull to let no need go unmet, to hover, was exactly the same as it had been back then. As I drove home, the memory of that Christmas we nearly lost Jeremy began to play again in my mind.

Jeremy had been sick for two days. There was a flu epidemic in town and hundreds of children were affected. At our pediatrician's office there was barely anywhere to sit. He insisted that Jeremy had the flu. He'd always run high fevers. "I don't think it's the flu," I said hesitantly, knowing physicians don't like Mom's diagnoses. He was adamant.

That night was even worse than the night before. I was up most of the night; Jerry got up often too. Jeremy appeared lethargic, his screams finally reduced to whimpers. When his fever hit 105 degrees,

I bundled him up, phoned the emergency room and drove him there. The nurse phoned our doctor, who said he could have a "fever shot," but nothing else. I desperately wanted penicillin for him.

I barely slept that night. When I did, I dreamed that a deadly tornado was heading for our house and Jerry and I were trying to get the children to safety. It was too close—we weren't going to make it. We shouted above the screaming wind, but couldn't hear each other.

By Saturday morning, a week before Christmas, Jeremy's head was swollen to enormous proportions and a little "thing" on his cheek had turned into a bluish abscess. I called a neighbor to stay with the other children, and Jerry and I dressed hurriedly and drove to the pediatrician's office. We didn't talk; words made it worse. Jeremy wasn't crying. He was still and quiet—much too still and quiet. We arrived at the doctor's office before it opened and waited. *Lord, how can we be sitting here waiting and he's not moving?* We knew the doctor was in for a very short time on Saturday mornings.

Finally—finally—we were in the examining room with him. Still, almost no words were spoken. He told us to take Jeremy to the hospital just across the street. I had prayed that he'd give him a penicillin shot, or go with us.

At the hospital, I ran past the admitting desk with Jeremy sleeping limply in my arms. I didn't even wait for an elevator, but ran up several flights of steps, with Jerry close behind me. At the pediatric floor, I burst through the door and screamed, "Somebody help us."

Help appeared from everywhere. Then Jerry and I were in a tiny examining room with Jeremy lying very still on a steel table, his eyes closed. Someone asked, "Do we have any orders?" Someone else asked, "Is the doctor coming?" Someone pulled Jeremy's eyelids up; his eyes had rolled back into his head. "I can't get a vein—they've collapsed," a nurse said. "Temperature is 106.4," someone whispered—but I heard.

Thoughts roared through my head like a runaway freight train. *He's dead. I only have one twin. This shouldn't have happened. He needs penicillin. Please don't let him be dead, God. Please.* Jerry held my hand so tightly that my fingers felt broken, but it didn't matter. Our pastor slipped into the already crowded room and prayed aloud.

A nurse rushed in. She worked in ICU, but today she'd been assigned to the pediatric floor—or else she was an angel dressed like a nurse. I can still see her face. Short wavy blond hair, cat's eye–shaped glasses, no smile but oh so determined and efficient-looking. *Thank You, God—whatever the outcome, thank You. She's going to do something.* She grabbed Jeremy, his naked body flopping like a rag doll. He was a big strong baby. I remember thinking: *I'm glad he's not frail, that he's a good eater.* His head bobbed as she ran with him, and I almost smiled at his beautiful red hair. She stopped at a large stainless steel sink and put him in it. All of us in the examining room followed her. Running. Hoping. She grabbed ice from the ice machine and began to pack him in it and barked at me, "Get ice on his head. *Now!*"

Oh, finally, I can do something. I held the ice cubes on his unbelievably hot head as it bobbled around in the crook of my arm. Others piled on ice. I think we all held our breath. I did.

Seconds ticked by and his little form looked hopeless. *Thank you, nurse. Even if he's dead, I see how hard you're trying. Bless you.*

Then suddenly, the most beautiful sound in the world: Jeremy screamed long and hard and loud.

Only then did I cry and say out loud, "Oh, thank You, Lord. He's back. Thank You."

He was placed in a little iron baby bed in a private room and almost immediately stood up and laughed out loud. They gave him a bottle and he began gulping it down. By then, orders had arrived for penicillin injections to begin immediately.

His first words, as he looked around the room at all of us beaming at him, were, "Whe bro?"—"Where's my brother?"

Our doctor arrived at our room after dark that day. "Is he better?" he asked with a laugh. Jerry jumped up out of his chair and greeted the doctor warmly and made conversation. I turned toward the window, wanting nothing to do with him and his light-hearted conversation and ridiculous grin.

I refused to leave Jeremy, staying by his side night and day. I wouldn't even leave him with Jerry. When I became exhausted and the nurses begged me to go home, I refused. I stood guard over him like a mother tiger. As I guarded him, bitterness began devouring the gratitude that had filled my heart. I didn't want it, but what I wanted didn't seem to matter. The bitterness was in charge.

When I did sleep, I dreamed the whole scene over and awakened in terror. And I couldn't bring myself to look in the little examining room where his pulse had stopped. My resentment fastened on an intense hatred of that room. I wanted it torn out of the hospital.

Jerry tried to help me. "Forget it, Mannie," he said. "It's over. Jeremy's all right." I knew he had no bitterness about what happened; it was obvious in his face. His joy was apparent every time he walked into Jeremy's room and picked him up. All Jerry felt was gratitude. Why couldn't I feel it too?

I became silent, staring straight ahead and thinking that I'd never forgive the doctor. I was so withdrawn at one point that Jerry had our family physician come by to talk with me. After that I made an effort to pretend that things were better. But I didn't fool Jerry. "We have so much to be grateful for, Mannie," he would say over and over. I heard his voice, and I knew he was right and I was wrong, but this resentment was stronger than any emotion I'd ever been caught in. *Dear God, I hate the bitterness. I just want to feel gratitude. Forgive my bitterness—take it away somehow.*

Jeremy had been given the smallest wheelchair I'd ever seen, and he loved to be wheeled through the halls. It was just two days before Christmas now. A gingerbread tree stood by the elevator. We always stopped to look at it. I turned my head away from that tiny examining room each time we passed.

Most of the children in the hospital had gone home for Christmas. Only one remained besides Jeremy. I peeked into her room, next to his, late in the afternoon. A small black girl looked out at us, then looked away.

"Hi," I said, smiling at her.

She wouldn't look at me. I read her name on the door. "Rosemary?" She glanced my way again. "If you ever want to come out and stroll with us, we'd love to have you." I saw a small wheelchair in the corner of her room. The next morning I came out of Jeremy's room. Rosemary sat there by our door in her wheelchair waiting for us.

"Hey, Rosemary." She didn't answer but began rolling her chair to keep up with us. I talked to her but didn't know if she heard me or could even speak. She seemed almost in a trance. Soon a nurse came and put her back into bed.

"How is she?" I asked the nurse when we were alone. She shook her head and looked away. "Will she be all right?" I persisted.

"She's retarded and a cripple. Has severe kidney problems and about four other major illnesses. She's in and out of here all the time."

"What are her chances?"

The nurse shook her head and looked away again, leaving hurriedly.

I followed her. "Do her parents come often?"

"Can't. They have other children, and they both work. They're probably trying to . . . detach . . ."

"But tomorrow's Christmas."

The nurse ran to answer the phone.

Throughout the day I'd go outside Jeremy's door and find Rosemary waiting. I learned to recognize the squeak of her chair. That evening I went out and found her. "Want to come watch me bathe Jeremy?"

She smiled faintly and nodded her head. I was overjoyed. I helped her to get her small wheelchair into the tiny bathroom. I was holding Jeremy on my lap, sitting on the edge of the tub as I ran the water. He was eager to get into the water, and it was difficult to hold him.

"Let me hold Jeremy for you," Rosemary offered suddenly, smiling. It was the first time she'd spoken.

Even before I looked up, I knew I must not hesitate. I simply couldn't do that with this child, so I said brightly, casually, I hoped, "Thank you, Rosemary. Hold him tight. He's strong."

She reached her thin arms up for Jeremy, and he reached back for her as though they were old friends. Instantly, she encircled him with both arms, holding him close and secure. Jeremy relaxed and snuggled close to her, holding onto one of her fat pigtails.

"I'll take him now, Rosemary. Thanks a lot."

She smiled proudly. "You're welcome."

After Jeremy and Rosemary were asleep, I asked one of the nurses if I could have Jerry bring Rosemary some presents for Christmas. She seemed pleased.

Jerry said he could get some toys as well as fruit and candy. Suddenly, I thought of something. "See if the girls mind if you bring their talking doll. She's just like new."

It was a strange Christmas Eve. I was without my family, and it didn't feel like Christmas and the hospital halls didn't smell like Christmas. They were quiet and nearly empty and smelled faintly of alcohol. I looked out Jeremy's window at the lights below and the Christmas trees—and the starry sky. That night I slept soundly, not even waking to check on Jeremy.

Jerry arrived early with the gifts. When I gave Rosemary the doll, she pulled the string in its back and the doll asked, "What is the color of my dress? Can you tie your shoes?" Rosemary's face glowed with joy. She hugged the doll to her.

Shortly after that our doctor came in, wished us a Merry Christmas and said that Jeremy was being released. He had been the victim of Ludwig's angina, a rare infection—one the doctors hadn't seen in more than fifteen years—that swells a victim's throat shut so no air can get through.

Jerry went to the office to settle Jeremy's bill. The doctor left without my speaking to him. I had turned and begun packing Jeremy's things. Then I picked up Jeremy, and we went to say good-bye to Rosemary.

"You goin' home, Jeremy Boy! You be good to your mama, you hear? You gon' be just fine."

I sat on the edge of her bed and hugged her with one arm, restraining Jeremy with the other. Still, he grabbed a pigtail and laughed. When I got it away from him, he latched onto Rosemary's doll. I attempted to take it away, but he held on tightly. "Let him have it," Rosemary said, smiling right at Jeremy.

"No, she's yours, Rosemary."

"But I want to give Jeremy something for Christmas."

"Oh, honey, you've given Jeremy so much—and me too. I couldn't have made it without you." I handed the doll back. "I'll keep her then. I named her Katherine. Do you like that name?"

"I love it."

I had to go, but I couldn't seem to leave. "Thank you for helping me, Rosemary."

"You're welcome."

I just stood there looking at a little girl with no future, holding onto a doll and smiling. Then I hurried from her room and walked briskly down the hall. I didn't look at the tree, though. I stopped stock still and looked directly into that tiny examining room. I stared long and hard.

Bitterness had vanished, and my heart pounded with overwhelming gratitude. *Oh, thank You, Lord, for Jeremy. Thank You—*

As I pushed the button for the elevator, the mechanical questions floated down the empty hall, "Can you tie your shoes? What is the color of my dress?"

My Father, I still remember praying in that tiny examining room when it appeared that Jeremy had died. My prayer was only one word: Please. *Against all odds, You allowed him to live. And now my prayer for Jeremy and his brother is just that one word:* Please. *I trust that someday You will give me two words to pray for them:* Thank You.

12 | TWO OF EVERYTHING BUT ME

DURING THE DRIVE BACK to Watkinsville from Mulberry Grove, other memories of Jeremy and Jon stood waiting at the door of remembrance.

There was the memory of that Christmas Day in 1968 when Jerry drove us back from the hospital to our home in Athens with a healthy nine-month-old Jeremy in my arms. I felt his weight in my arms and smelled his hair and kissed him over and over and talked softly to him. This would always be the most wonderful Christmas Day of my life.

And there was the day the previous March when I'd left the same hospital to bring home my newborn twins. They were just four days old, but they were big: five pounds ten ounces and six pounds thirteen ounces. Jeremy was the larger baby. I'd carried him up high, breach, and Jon in the natural position. The doctors had thought they'd come early, like most twins. But they didn't even arrive in the month they were due.

Jon and Jeremy missed being leap-year babies by a little over two hours and arrived on March 1. I'd been expecting girls again—I'd name them Jessica and Johanna. Back then no one knew what she was having until the baby actually arrived. At seven months, an X-ray had shown that I was expecting twins. Jerry and I and, of course, Julie and Jennifer were thrilled.

I'd thought we were ready for twins. We had two of *every-*

thing. Friends had been especially generous at my baby shower. I expected to sail through being the mother of four children, just as I had as the mother of two.

When I came to in the recovery room (in the dark ages before epidurals), a smiling nurse said, "Congratulations, Mrs. West. You have two big boys."

For a moment I didn't say anything. My thinking was still a bit fuzzy. "Are you sure? I expected girls."

"Well, that's not what you got," she answered, not smiling quite as much.

"Boys?" I said, raising myself up on one elbow.

"Yes," she said adamantly. "Do you wish to see them?"

"Oh yes. Yes, of course! Do they weigh enough?"

While she and another nurse went to get my babies, I reasoned: *Well, boys can't be that different from girls. I'll dress them in little knee pants with suspenders and long socks. It'll be fun . . .*

Oh, how much I had to learn!

The nurse carrying Jeremy showed him to me first. Like all my children, he had red fuzz for hair and looked amazingly like his father. Then they showed me Jonathan. He didn't look like Jeremy or Julie or Jennifer or Jerry or me—or anybody I'd ever seen. "They don't match." I bellowed.

"They are fraternal, Mrs. West. Just brothers born at the same time."

"But Jeremy looks just like Julie and Jennifer, and Jonathan doesn't look like—anybody. He looks worried—like an old man. Are you sure that . . ."

She held his little foot up to show me the band on it that matched one of the two on my arm. She wasn't smiling at all.

From the beginning I was disappointed that they weren't

identical. My daughters had often been mistaken for twins, and now that I actually had twins, they didn't even look alike. In retrospect, I can't imagine why I thought that way. But I did.

I was to discover that they weren't identical in disposition either. I could never get them on the same schedule—they ate hours apart and took naps at different times. They demanded different kinds of food. Jon's "worried" look continued to bother me, just as it had when I first saw him. He weighed much less than the other three children, and his face wasn't as filled out.

When they were seventeen months old, Jeremy learned how to climb out of his bed. When he got out, he'd free Jon, usually at about six in the morning. Together they'd open their window, knock the screen out and jump to the ground—in their little blue pajamas with feet. They were about twenty-five pounds each, and fifty pounds of babies can do about whatever they want.

Our phone would ring at 6:05 A.M., and the little lady at the end of the street who had no children of her own would say in a chipper voice, "Hello, Marion dear. Your boys are loose again. They're in my yard." Her yard was a thing of beauty. I'd run out of my house, sometimes able to grab a robe, and rescue them. Somehow, Jerry was always in the shower when the calls came.

One day I told Jerry, "If you don't fix Jeremy's bed so he can't get out, I—I—I don't know who's going to take care of all these children anymore." I knew I didn't mean it, but I intended to get his attention.

That night he came home from work with a roll of chicken wire under one arm and a sack of nails in the other. He pulled the sides of Jeremy's bed up all the way and nailed the chicken wire neatly around it. We both stood back and smiled as he put Jeremy down into the pen/bed. Then we watched in disbelief as Jeremy climbed up the chicken wire, hopped down onto the floor, and ran down the hall. I remembered what one of the hospital nursery workers had told me when the boys were born: "You can tell a lot about children by just watching them here in the nursery. I can tell you that your Jeremy is going to give you a run for your money."

Jerry got a ladder and put the chicken wire all the way across the top of the bed. He made a little trapdoor that opened and shut easily, with hinges and a tiny lock. He slid Jeremy in through the door and locked it. "Don't you ever leave him in there longer than two hours at a time," he warned me.

I nodded. Actually, Jeremy was delighted with the cage-bed. He sat down and laughed and poked his fingers through the holes, amused and entertained.

That was just a preview of coming attractions. Jeremy could climb over a chain link fence at two, which meant no nursery school would take the boys for a couple of mornings a week. Once he discovered the storm drain out by our house, a new underground world opened up for him. One day he and Jonathan disappeared while I was in the bathroom. We finally located them underground—we could hear them laughing. They were way back in the huge pipe, almost to our backyard!

I spent a lot of time sitting in the yard watching them. I'd read some too. Jeremy would climb a huge tree while Jon stood at the bottom yelling for him to come down. He climbed like a monkey, so I finally just let him. More than once, people stopped and screamed, "Lady, your child is at the top of that tree. Just sit still. I'll call for help." Then I had to explain that he knew how to come down and he was fine. Today I'd probably have been reported to Child Welfare.

Another thing Jeremy loved to do was to open the car door and swing out on it while I was driving. Car seats were optional back then, and even after we got them, Jeremy would climb out and do his swinging-on-the-car-door trick, which horrified bystanders as well as me.

One day I was at the kitchen sink washing dishes and watching the twins playing just outside. By then Jerry had fenced in the yard; when Jeremy started to climb the fence, I had time to go retrieve him. Once I tied them securely to our long clothesline in their baby blue harnesses and gave them the run of the entire backyard. But this particular day, they were running free with our dog Muff. She'd bark if anything went wrong. It was almost lunch time, and I heard Jon say, "Brother, go ask Mama for cookies."

"No, you go," Jeremy insisted.

"You," Jon said, "If I ask, she'll say no. But she'll give them to you."

Jeremy came through the backdoor and said, "Mama, give us some cookies."

And I did, and I made myself face the truth: I wouldn't have given them to Jon. *What kind of mother was I anyway?*

Jeremy liked to invent things, and I liked the creativity he expressed. At Christmas he usually put aside the toys and made things with the boxes they came in. Once, in the grocery store, he escaped from the grocery cart, and I knew somewhere he was hiding in a box. The trouble was, that day they were tossing out cardboard boxes, and I had to go to the manager. Jon sat in the buggy looking worried about his brother.

Then the announcement came over the loudspeaker: "Shoppers, there's a little boy with red hair hiding in a box. Everyone be on the lookout for him, and no one throw away any boxes until he's found."

Jeremy laughed all the way home. He could curl up into an amazingly small ball and fit himself into the smallest box in the world. But he loved big boxes too. If rain set in, I'd have Jerry pick up a refrigerator box from Georgia Power, where he worked. Both Jon and Jeremy would entertain themselves for hours with it. I hated the way it looked in the den, but at least I knew they were safe. Jeremy also rescued things from trash cans. Chewing gum wrappers, sticks, leaves, a crust of bread, a discarded bottle were all treasures. And he worked methodically making things out of them. He adored them, but Jon wasn't interested in them at all.

Jeremy took more chances, disappeared from the yard faster, and required more attention than Jon. Before I realized what was happening, Jon became an outsider. In retrospect, I see it clearly. At the time, it wasn't so obvious.

Lying in bed on a dismal, rainy morning in 1970, I didn't see how I could survive another day with my boys. I couldn't understand what had gone wrong. How had I failed so miserably? Growing up, all I'd wanted to be was a mother. Even though I was an only child, I dreamed of having lots of children, over whom I'd preside full of smiles and fun. When I met and married Jerry, my dreams seemed on their way to coming true.

Now I spent all my time trying to avert disaster, worn out before the day began. That rainy morning, after waving the girls off to school, I flopped back down on the bed, too depressed to budge. There was a moment of silence, which was usually a signal that the twins were up to something, then a loud crash. *What now?*

I raced into the kitchen. Jeremy was standing on the stove while Jon waited expectantly below, the breakfast cereal bowls overturned at his feet. Before I could intervene, Jeremy wrenched open a cabinet and threw down an open bag of sugar. Spotting me, he leaped to the floor like a chimpanzee, and both boys began licking sugar off the linoleum.

A dull headache began in my temples and spread to the back of my neck. Out the kitchen window, I caught a glimpse of my neighbor and two other friends stepping outside to go shopping, the three women smiling under their brightly colored umbrellas. *Their* children were in school. They could do all they wanted from nine till three. It seemed like an eternity before my sons would be off to kindergarten. Would I ever smile again? Would I ever hop into a car with friends just to go someplace for fun?

By now Jon and Jeremy were working on the lower cabinet locks. "Boys," I screamed, "stop it!" As I knelt with a sponge to clean up the mess, Jon and Jeremy banged pots and pans together gleefully.

Why hadn't anyone warned me how messy and exasperating motherhood could be? In TV shows and in the magazines I read, mothers were capable and self-confident. They spoke in soft, gentle tones like my own mother. They never screamed.

Somehow I made it through the day, but by the time Julie and Jennifer came through the door, shaking the water off their yellow raincoats, I was spent. Everywhere I stepped there were crumbs, crayons, flattened raisins. As the girls entertained their brothers, I wearily started supper.

That night after another hectic meal, Jerry started to take the garbage out.

"Stop," I shouted. "I haven't been anywhere in two years. Tonight I'm going out to the trash can—and I'm going alone."

Lord, Jon and Jeremy were never supposed to match. You knit them together perfectly before they were born. How I wish I could have understood that back then! I thought motherhood was too hard. My children surely thought childhood was too hard, especially Jon. You are forgiving; so are my children. Help me to forgive myself.

13 | GLORY AT THE GARBAGE CAN

JON AND JEREMY HAD BEEN JUST TWO that night I fled from the kitchen and "ran away" to the garbage can, leaving a surprised Jerry, Julie and Jennifer staring as I picked up the trash, marched out the door and kicked it shut. The boys were under the table, or on it, or somewhere they didn't belong. I had to have a moment of quiet; I had to be alone, if only for a little while.

I stood in my backyard, holding two overflowing sacks of garbage. I held them tightly, not wanting to dump them into the trash container. Then I would have to go back into the house.

I felt like part of the garbage, and almost wished I could jump in with it and have someone put the lid back on the can.

The coldness of the night was delicious. I shivered and inhaled deeply. For just a few moments I was alone. I savored the privacy.

I didn't want to go back in there, to a house with four children. In spite of Jerry's being a good husband and our having a nice home, I felt like a failure. I felt I could no longer cope with being a mother—all I'd ever wanted to be. Why had no one warned me that it could be so very difficult? I felt as though every day and night was a nightmare that I screamed my way through.

Each day loomed ahead like an eternity. I resented all the demands that the boys made and hated myself for it. I was desperately tired. I hadn't know motherhood would involve every minute of every day—and still the children would demand more. At least the boys would. The girls tried so hard not to ask for anything.

I liked things neat and orderly and on schedule. As an only child, I was used to having privacy. Now I couldn't even have my own Scotch tape or pencils. And even after twelve years of marriage, I couldn't get used to picking up after everyone.

The twins were unusually active and destructive. Two ladies from the church stopped by one day. I had been absent from services for quite a while. Jerry went and took the girls, I stayed home with Jon and Jeremy and cooked lunch.

The women had just come from the beauty shop. Maids were cleaning their homes. Their children were almost grown. Now they were going shopping and out to lunch. But they had come by to tell me they missed me at church. They wanted to know why I hadn't been coming.

Old blankets covered the brick hearth where Jon and Jeremy often pushed each other down. They had removed the tubes from the television. There were no curtains in the den because they had pulled down both the curtains and the rods. We had to move so many things out of the room that there was an echo as we talked. Toys were scattered across the floor, along with empty cereal boxes. Dirty diapers were stacked in the bathroom.

It was so good to have adults to talk with, but as soon as we sat down the boys crawled into the fireplace and began reaching up the chimney, getting their hands black. I snatched both of them, holding one between my knees and the other in my arms. They arched their backs and screamed for freedom.

The visit lasted about six minutes. "How do you stand it?" one of the ladies asked in open honesty as they were leaving.

"I'd go crazy," the other said with a laugh as they both encouraged me to come back to Sunday school and church. As I watched them drive away, tears slid down my face. *I can't stand it either. I'm going crazy.*

I looked at the mess I'd live in all day and wondered: *How can I be the same person who just a few years ago never had a thing out of place?*

I was becoming chilled as I stood in my dark backyard and looked at the lights in the neighborhood. *I'm failing,* I thought. *How can I fail at something as important as motherhood? I can't fail and I don't know how to succeed. I'm caught in the middle. I just want out.*

I was about to cry, and I didn't want to. *I have to go back inside. That's my world in there.* I pictured my kitchen: supper dishes to be washed; two highchairs caked in sticky crumbs and spilled milk; and a floor littered with gummy food. In the den there were books, toys, cookie crumbs, pots and pans, torn magazines, everyone's shoes. When these were gathered up, a mountain of diapers waited to be folded. Jon and Jeremy must be bathed and forced into pajamas. They would struggle, making a game out of it. Julie and Jennifer would be waiting for Jerry to help them with their math.

A little part of me still cried out silently, *Jerry, please, let's talk in a room where there isn't a thing that looks childlike.* But most of me insisted, *What's the use? By the time all the children are satisfied and in bed, I'll have fallen across my bed asleep in my clothes and Jerry won't be able to wake me.*

I loved sleep. It relieved me of all responsibility of doing anything for anyone. But it only lasted a short time. I'd learned to hate mornings. Everybody wanted something at the same time. And there were two wet, hungry, destructive, jabbering twins to satisfy all day long.

Almost numb from the cold, I delayed going back into the house. Still holding the overflowing garbage, I looked up at the sky. It was beautiful. I hadn't appreciated beauty in so long. But I had four beautiful children. There was Orion—just like it used to be when I was a little girl and my girlfriend and I lay on a quilt to watch falling stars. Was there really ever a time when I had all the freedom I wanted and when I wasn't tired?

I sobbed out loud. There were no children to watch me. I wasn't used to the privacy. Looking up at the stars and sky I realized with absolute certainty something I'd known for a long time: *There's a God, all right. He exists. He's just forgotten about me. If only I could get His attention. How does one get God's attention? Does everyone but me who goes to church have something I've missed?* I was going down for the third time and I wanted to be pulled back up to happiness. I wanted to smile again—at my husband and my children and myself.

Still looking at the sky and hoping desperately that He was listening, without even shutting my eyes or bowing my head, I cried out desperately, "I'm not going to make it, Lord."

I knew in my heart my prayer meant more than what I'd said out loud. I was saying, *I can't do it. Look down, see me. Help me. I need You, God. I give up.*

Nothing changed immediately. There were no burning bushes or fifteen-foot-tall angels. No fireworks. But I had called out to God, and I should have realized that He had heard me. He had a plan, but back then I couldn't see it—even while it was unfolding.

Father, I know You do some mighty works in churches. I've seen them. But with me, it usually seems to be just You and me in somewhat unusual locations. I'll never forget that desperate night when the very God of heaven came down from the throne room and met with a mother falling apart—by the garbage can!

SURRENDERED AND SET FREE | 14

I EXPECTED THINGS TO BE DIFFERENT the next day. After all, I'd asked for help. But when Jerry and the girls left that morning, the familiar sense of panic closed in. I couldn't bear to be inside for a minute more. I bundled the twins into their sweaters and strapped them in the stroller. As we were walking around the block, we ran into some other mothers coming back from school. We chatted briefly, then one of the women jotted down a telephone number on a slip of paper and handed it to me.

"It's the number of someone who counsels mothers having a hard time. In case you ever need to call her, Marion," she said. "It's a free service with the University of Georgia."

"Thanks," I said, mortified. Did I look that frazzled? I took the paper and shoved it into my pocket, thinking I'd tear it up as soon as I got home. The mothers I read about always handled things on their own. I would too.

But as I continued down the block, I wondered if I was too quick in my dismissal of counseling. Was I too proud to admit I was having trouble coping? I had prayed to God for help. Maybe this was the very help He was offering.

At home I pulled out the scrap of paper and read, "Dr. Laura Levine, Rutland Center," and a telephone number. I picked up my kitchen phone. I didn't want to call anyone. I didn't want to admit what a failure I was. Anyway, what would

I say to a counselor? Tell her that I was a terrible mother? I put down the phone.

There was a tremendous crash. Jon and Jeremy appeared at the door, each one lugging half of the top of the toilet tank. They had somehow broken it in two, and laughed triumphantly as if bearing a trophy. The whole scene was so awful and absurd that I almost saw it as a sure sign from God.

Pick up the phone and call. Now. You must do this now!

Cradling the receiver under my chin, I wiped the boys' hands with a tissue where they had scratched their fingers, and then I dialed the number. I tried to sound casual as I spoke to the assistant, but my mouth went dry and I stumbled over my words. After I explained my situation, they gave me an appointment for Thursday, three days away. *If I can survive until then!*

Thursday finally arrived. I brought the boys with me as instructed. A young assistant with a reassuring smile took them to the playroom. I was ushered into an office where a woman with pearls and a smart gray suit greeted me warily. Sitting across from her desk, I was afraid she could hear my heart pounding as I told her how I felt.

Dr. Levine told me that I must get away from my sons for short periods of time. "Can you and your husband arrange to put Jon and Jeremy into a good nursery school two half-days a week?"

What? And not be a perfect full-time mother? I was horrified at the thought.

Dr. Levine read my expression. She leaned across the desk and calmly said, "If you don't do this, I can't help you. No one can. It's what you need to do for yourself." Her words were so strong they startled me. It was as if God were saying, *You asked for help. Well, here it is.*

Back home, Jerry agreed with her suggestion and I started looking for nursery schools. I was turned down by two of them when I explained that Jeremy could easily climb over a chain-link fence. But a third accepted the boys and then, to my delight, they seemed to adore it.

Still unsure of what I should do with my newfound freedom, I volunteered at the hospital, signing up for a new program called Recreational Therapy. I found myself enjoying it, and when I talked to the other volunteers, I was almost afraid to tell them that this wasn't work for me at all. It was a vacation from my children.

One day at lunch with four other volunteers, someone asked, "How are your kids, Marion?"

"My husband had to build a cage out of chicken wire to keep Jeremy in his bed," I blurted out. What would they think of me now?

To my surprise, they all laughed. "My sister-in-law had to have one of those things too," one woman remarked. "It worked beautifully."

As the women continued with stories of their own, I related more tales of the twins. But now, feeling less claustrophobic, I could actually see the comedy of it: the spilled sugar, the banging pots and pans, the broken toilet top. It was like swapping war stories, and I was happy that I had some good ones. I felt relieved and even a little proud of myself. It wasn't so bad not being a perfect mom after all. My hyperactive kids weren't the problem; the expectations I had of myself were.

After work I picked up the boys from nursery school, and we sang "Old MacDonald" all the way home. When the girls came home, they found us sitting under the weeping willow making mud pies. The house was a mess, but I knew immediately what we should do. "Let's go on a picnic," I suggested.

"Really?" Julie and Jennifer screamed joyfully. I threw some hot dogs, chips and cookies into a picnic basket. Never mind that there was dried milk on the kitchen floor, toys all over the den, and a mountain of laundry by the washing machine. We piled into the station wagon—even our dog, Muff. I drove to a nearby spot, and we scrambled out of the car and into a meadow.

"Mama, look at all the flowers up on the hill!" Jennifer said. As the kids dashed off to gather daisies, I said a silent prayer of thanks that I'd picked up the phone.

Meanwhile, friends from my Sunday school class had been phoning weekly to say, "We miss you." I resented it. I resented that they got to check on their offering envelopes that they'd made a contact—me, the shut-in. I had no idea they really cared and were praying for me regularly.

I believe that because of that night at the garbage can, God had one of my friends secretly call Jerry. She'd said, "We're really concerned about Marion. We want her to hear a speaker we're having on Tuesday night. We'll come by and pick her up. You just get her to the car, okay? We invited her, but she refused."

Jerry agreed quickly.

On Tuesday night all the children ran to see who had driven up. I didn't even tell them to come away from the window. Jerry took me by the hand and said, "You're going to a meeting with some of your friends."

"I am not!" I screamed, getting a look at myself in the mirror. As I struggled, he put me in the car while four little faces peered out the window. Then the car roared off like something out of *Bonnie and Clyde.*

My friends dragged me out of the car and inside a lovely home. It was full of people; everyone came up to greet me, and then someone introduced the speaker of the evening: beautiful, poised, a smart dresser, with a radiant smile, a soothing voice, and laughing eyes. I wanted to crawl out the door. *She's probably got one well-behaved child, a full-time maid, and a huge house, and her mother lives next door.*

Huh? She had four children, their house was too small like ours, no maid. She, too, had been a weary mother, but she'd met this new friend. I half listened, sitting on the floor because the room was so crowded. She was so wonderful that I thought, *I may just throw up all over this new baby blue carpet.*

And then Tricia Jones, smiling from ear to ear, her beautiful blond hair bouncing around, said, "I want all of you to meet my new friend."

I thought: *Well, super-duper. The minister of music will jump out of a closet, and we'll sing something from a hymnal, and then I can go home.*

She absolutely glowed when she announced, "He's a person— the Lord Jesus Christ. . . ."

Person?

She talked about her personal relationship with Jesus and how He had changed *everything.* She didn't even mind picking up her husband's shorts anymore.

At home in bed, I thought before going to sleep, *Is she for real?* I'd joined the church and been baptized when I was nine, like all my friends. Jerry and I attended church and moved our membership every time Georgia Power transferred him. We went on Wednesday nights, and Sunday nights too. Jerry was even Sunday school superintendent. And I'd worked in the two-year-old department.

For the next two years, I attended the Bible study taught by Tricia Jones in the basement of a large home. They had a nursery. At first, maybe I just went to have someone to look after the boys so I could be with grown-ups. But then I started looking forward to those Thursdays.

More and more I wondered, *Do I know that person, the Lord Jesus Christ?*

One week in early March—the twins were four—it must have rained for forty days and forty nights. We never got to go outside, and the boys were almost climbing the walls—me too. Then they got interested in the refrigerator box Jerry had brought home during his lunch hour. They played back in their room, and I had some alone time in the den.

I began to think about how all my life I'd wanted my own way. Now I wanted a new house because we needed a larger one. I wanted to be a good mother, but. . . .

Suddenly, more than anything in the world I wanted peace. I felt that I was standing on the brink of a huge decision I could no longer delay, as if I were about to jump off a cliff, having been told that someone would catch me. But how could I know unless I jumped? Someone has said that prayer is an attitude of the heart. I came to understand those words a little better that day—March 4, 1972.

My heart cried out: *I don't care what it costs. It doesn't matter anymore. I want You, God, in total control of my life, no matter what happens. Take the last five percent of me that I've held back. I give it to You now—I give me to You. Forgive all my dishonesty and sin. Let's do things Your way. I've called You Lord, but You have never been my Lord. I so want to know the Lord Jesus Christ. I want a personal relationship with Him, I really do. I surrender everything— wanting to be a writer, to be Georgia Mother of the Year* (yes, I'd wanted that), *wanting a new house. . . .*

I felt an outpouring of love that just wouldn't stop. It was the sweetest thing I've ever known in my life. "Thank You for loving me, Lord," I said. Suddenly, all the old hymns I'd sung as a child made sense—spiritual sense. "Nothing but the blood," "Jesus, Jesus, Jesus, sweetest name I know," "I surrender all," "Just as I am," "Have thine own way, Lord," and the new song that I loved so much. It was actually an ancient hymn, but somehow new to me. . . . "Out of my bondage, sorrow and night, Jesus, I come, Jesus, I come. . . ."

I could feel myself smiling, and I hadn't smiled for so long. I ran to the mirror and sure enough, I was smiling from ear to ear—just like Tricia Jones!

Suddenly, I loved my little crowded house with the worn wallpaper and spots on the carpet and the fingerprints all over the walls. I walked outside and looked up in the blue sky and this thought came to me powerfully like a letter from God: *You don't have a single problem or guilt or worry. I, your Lord and Maker, have taken them all. Trust Me daily, Marion.*

One of the most amazing things about this surrender experience was that for the very first time, I really liked Marion and accepted myself just as I was. Most of my life I'd wanted to be like somebody else. I wanted to wear size five-and-a-half shoes instead of eight-and-a-half. I wanted to be five feet five inches, not five seven. I longed for naturally curly hair and flawless skin like Snow White—and a turned-up nose. How I longed to be able to play the piano and sing on key and enjoy being a hostess! I wanted to be a smiling mother like the ones in books and never scream at my children. My list seemed endless. I wanted a golden tan and lots of matching clothes. I wanted, I wanted, I wanted . . .

It's an amazing thing to suddenly like yourself, just as you are, and to thank God for the way He made you. Later I'd realize that liking myself permitted me to forget about self, and that's a real victory—one that has been a long time coming for me.

Two weeks later Jerry got a marvelous promotion, and we went house hunting in the Atlanta area. I'd made a list before my "surrender" of all the things I wanted in a house. Now it truly didn't matter. "We can live in a tree house," I told my astonished husband, who still couldn't figure out what had happened to me. I thought God told me just to be quiet about it for a while.

The last house we looked at, in Lilburn, was the house I'd seen in my mind. Even the wallpaper I'd picked out was there, the four bedrooms, a recreation room, plus a den, a huge country kitchen in avocado (it was the era of gold and avocado) and a fenced backyard. It was all there!

When the dishwasher overflowed after our move, I remembered something Tricia had taught in Bible study: Praise God for bad things, not just good things. So I sat down on the floor with crossed legs, all the children around me, and prayed, "Lord, I thank You that I have someone to wash dishes for, that we even have a dishwasher, that we have running water, that I'm not going to panic over this." The children sat down too, and we all stared at the water running from the dishwasher. A neighbor happened by and suggested I look in the J-shaped pipe under the sink. I did, and there were four knives. She helped me put the pipe back together, and the dishwasher drained properly while I mopped up the water and did a little dance around the kitchen as the children watched, speechless.

The experience was so moving that I sat down and hurriedly wrote an article about it, with my usual number of misspelled words, and mailed it to the inspirational magazine *Guideposts*.

It was accepted. I called it "Thank You, Lord, for My Broken Dishwasher." Other articles were accepted, and while I wasn't elected Georgia Mother of the Year, the joy that hung around me was almost more than I could believe.

I finally thought I understood: When we give to God the thing we want desperately, He has a unique way, many times, of turning around and presenting it to us as a gift—with His blessings. He does love to give good gifts to His children!

We'd been living in Lilburn for a while when I took out the trash one night. It was spring and the sweet smell of honeysuckle drifted by. Crickets sang their night song in syncopated rhythm. I stood very still in the moonlight and gazed up at the sky. Orion had never shone more beautifully.

I knew—oh, how I knew—that God had reached down and touched me at my trash can back in Athens and set me free. He'll meet with anyone, anytime, anyplace.

Smiling, I hurried back inside.

Oh, Father, pride is so ugly. I think I've hidden it and You are able to see it all along. Maybe others see it too. I was too proud to ask for help. Help me remember that "Help me, Lord" is a good prayer, especially for mothers—especially for me.

PART FOUR

"AND THE FIELDS
PRODUCE NO FOOD . . ."

15 | THE BLUE HORSE TABLET OF LOVE

OUR NEW HOME was nearly three thousand square feet, and yet it was priced within our budget. Jerry drove to downtown Atlanta to his job at Georgia Power Company—an hour and a half each way in traffic. But he didn't complain. He never complained about anything.

Still, I thought since I'd had my mountaintop experience with God that there was a whole lot God needed to do to my husband. However, God just kept chipping away at me, it seemed. I was busy writing, then speaking too. I shared things I had no intention of sharing, things that didn't make me look very good as a mother or wife. But since I was depending on Him, I had to speak whatever He gave me or just be on my own.

One day He had me tell about something I never planned to share—ever.

Jon and Jeremy must have been in second grade when I lost it one morning with Jon. I still had trouble liking him—I loved him and did things for him, but I didn't understand him very well. He was always hungry, and things seemed to break whenever he entered a room. He whined a lot and talked loudly. He needed my attention on a one-on-one basis. I knew that, but wouldn't admit it. It's amazing how we can fool ourselves sometimes.

Jon wouldn't sit by me in church or share a hymnal with me,

only his daddy. They were really tight. He had recently stopped letting me tuck him into bed or give him a good-night hug. He wouldn't let me help him get the knots out of his shoelaces. He'd holler, "*Noooooo. Leave me alone.*" So I did.

I left him alone too much.

Early one morning when Jerry was out of town on business, I overslept. From our upstairs bedroom I heard loud noises in the kitchen. I hopped out of bed and flew down the stairs. I believe God sort of tapped me on the shoulder and offered, *Let Me help you. This is going to be very difficult.* In my heart, I said, *I can handle this.* So I was on my own when I rounded the corner in the kitchen, already angry and about to explode because of whatever was going on.

Jeremy was eating his cereal matter-of-factly. Jon, on the other hand, had poured a whole box of Cheerios into a huge container—I don't know what it was; it looked like a hubcap— and he was using a cooking spoon to torpedo into the cereal and milk. *Slosh, Splash. Zoom.*

I felt something explode inside me, and I was out of control— totally. I screamed, *"You are so dumb, stupid, and clumsy, and every-thing you do upsets me."*

Jon continued as though I were invisible, and I reached out to hit him. He was very quick and leaned back in his chair to avoid my hand and fell over backward. The bowl of cereal came with him and sloshed out all over him and the floor.

I stood over him screaming. He said what he always said: "It wasn't my fault." How I hated that sentence!

Just then I heard the squeak of the school bus outside and said, "Jeremy, there's the bus." Jeremy hopped up; I leaned down and gave him a kiss, and he ran out the door.

Jon stood up slowly. He looked like a giant Cheerio. They were stuck all over him. He tried to pull off a few of them. *"Get on the bus!"* I screamed.

Finally, he stammered, "Don't make me go to school— like this."

"Get on the bus!" I screamed again, wishing I could handle the situation differently, hating myself and Jon right then.

Jon almost never begged me for anything or said please. But his voice grew very soft, and he said, "Please, Mama." Tears sat in his fearful eyes.

"Go!" I bellowed.

He walked out the door, wiping his tears quickly with the back of his hand, never looking back.

Then he came running back. "Mama," he explained, "teacher said, 'If you don't have a Blue Horse tablet today, don't come to school.' I don't have one. I never have what I need. Jeremy always has what he needs . . ."

"Get on that bus!" I said between clenched teeth.

And he did.

All the words had tasted bitter and hot coming out of my mouth—the horrible words that I had no power to stop. I knew we weren't really talking about a tablet, although he probably was supposed to have one and hadn't told me.

What he was asking for was unconditional love. He knew it—and so did I.

Back in the house I sat down at the old oak kitchen table and put my head down on my arms. I'd never experienced such out-and-out defeat with no hope in sight. *How can this be happening to me? I don't deserve God's forgiveness, and I sure can't ask for it.*

You must ask, Marion. Just ask. You will be forgiven. What you deserve isn't important. Ask.

I couldn't, even in the silence of my heart. I didn't want to face God now. I wanted to crawl back in bed or under it. Then something happened: The icy pool of pride around my heart began to melt into a great pool of need, and I cried out, *Oh, Lord. Forgive me. Please forgive me, even though I don't deserve it. I ask for Your forgiveness. . . .*

You have it. Now ask Jon for forgiveness.

I will when he comes home.

No. I want you to go to school—now—and ask Jon's forgiveness.

I will when he comes home today.

No. Go to school now.

Get him out of class?

Yes. Hurry. It's the only way.

I don't know. . . .

But by then it was as if a magnet drew me to the school. Dressing quickly, I imagined Jon's surprised face when he saw me there. Up to this point, I'd never apologized to one of my children when I'd been wrong. As I backed the car out of the driveway, there seemed to be one more thing. *Stop by the store and pick up a Blue Horse tablet. A big one.*

Oh, Lord, You are so wonderful—and practical too. Go with me.

I plan to. Thank you for inviting Me.

There were thoughts of: *Stupid. Do you think God talks to you? Well, He doesn't. You're making all this up.*

I always heard the other voice when I thought God was speaking to me.

I'd only been hearing from God since that day in my den. I just had to choose to believe God and do what He said. I ran into a Quick Stop and bought an enormous Blue Horse tablet and then hurried on to school. At the principal's office, I said, "I need to speak to my son, Jon West, for a moment."

Someone announced over the intercom, "Jon West, come to the office now."

Jon was always being called to the office—I knew that. He probably thought he was in trouble again. Standing in the hall, I saw him approaching before he saw me.

Head down, shoes untied, shirt buttoned up wrong, looking totally defeated, he came anyway to whatever awaited him. As he got closer, I saw a couple of Cheerios still clinging to him.

Love for him so filled my heart that I had no doubt this had been God's idea, and that He waited alongside me to help me. I desperately needed His help.

Jon looked up suddenly and saw me. He saw my face and he must have seen clear inside to my broken heart. "Mom."

He came close. By now he saw the Blue Horse tablet in my hand, and his eyes went from my face to the tablet. I'd been preparing this marvelous speech—equivalent to the Gettysburg Address—but I couldn't speak. All I could do was stand there and love him—unconditionally.

As he looked up at me, I managed to say, "Jon, I love you so much. Will you forgive me?" My tears were landing all over the Blue Horse tablet.

"Sure, Mama. Sure." He said it quickly, thoroughly, honestly. Grateful for the opportunity, I handed him the tablet, and he marveled quietly as though I'd given him a ticket to Disney World. I knew the unwritten rule that forbids a mother to kiss her child in front of his peers; now Jon's were all around us. Still, I knelt down beside him and whispered, "Would you give me a little kiss?" I felt certain that's what God wanted me to do. I had no hope of Jon kissing me, of course. He wouldn't even let me hug him without a struggle.

He surprised me by locking his strong arms around my neck and giving me the first kiss on my nose. Right then I lost my balance, and we sat down together in the middle of the hall outside the principal's office. We embraced in a deadlock hug, and he continued kissing me, going all around my face. I lost count of the kisses as I held on to him, trying hard not to cry. It was bad enough that I was hugging him in the hall; I didn't want to cry too.

All his friends who walked by us looked up at the ceiling like there was something wonderful overhead to keep from staring at Jon. God worked out each detail of my apology.

When we both stood up he had his Blue Horse tablet under his arm. He let me tie his shoes while he buttoned his shirt correctly. I picked off a few stubborn remaining Cheerios, and we stood there smiling at each other.

Finally Jon said, "See ya. Thanks."

"Have a wonderful day, Jon!"

I watched him walk away, looking like a totally different child even from the back. He was bouncing, sort of, with his Blue Horse tablet under his arm. He looked like a little boy who was going to have a good day at school.

That afternoon after school Jon and Jeremy came charging into the kitchen. "Want to see my math paper, Mom?" Jon asked, smiling. He'd been failing math, but I resolved to say something like, "I'm sure you tried." He pulled a paper from his back pocket and unfolded it slowly, dramatically. One hundred! In big red letters, the teacher had written: "Jon really tried today and did beautiful work. I'm so proud of him!"

Me too. For the second time that day, I enfolded Jon in my arms.

Oh, Father, what a day! So much bad, so much good. You never give up on me and my mistakes as a mother. Thank You. Thank You for dear little Jon and his quickness to forgive—so much, for so long. Thank You for our "love-in" there in the school hall. Thank You that I see him differently. He's so fine, brave, strong. Thank You that I'm back in his life. Show me ways to encourage him, ways to express my love.

HINDS' FEET IN BASEBALL CLEATS | 16

WITH JEREMY SETTLED IN at Mulberry Estates Assisted Living and cared for, Gene and I concentrated on Jon, still in the hospital and having surgeries on his right hand. We continued to be grateful that he was left-handed.

One day when we walked into his room, he said, "Mom, I need some shoes. We went to the hospital so quick, I didn't put on shoes. Or maybe I did—but I could have left them in the emergency room. Anyway, I can't walk around barefoot."

I told him that I'd get him some shoes. As I talked to him, I reached down and touched one of his feet—the one with the big brown freckle on it. It had appeared when he was about three months old and looked exactly like one on my leg. Jon's feet were, well, so—pretty. Surely that's not the word for a man's feet. But they looked perfect, no blisters or skinned places, kind of like huge baby feet.

I really meant to get him some shoes, but I forgot, so the next time we visited, he showed me the brand-new sandals that some of his friends had brought him. He seemed genuinely proud of them. "Jesus sandals," he called them. They reminded me of something from his childhood.

Jerry was going out of town and had made me promise that I'd get Jon new cleats before the big game. "Okay," I answered from down in the laundry room where I was putting clothes in the dryer.

"I'm serious, Marion. You can't forget," he hollered up from the kitchen.

I purposely didn't answer. I was responsible.

In a couple of minutes Jerry stood in the door of the washroom. "Promise me," he said, as though we were talking about a blood transfusion instead of shoes.

"Okay, okay," I said, irritated.

"It's important, Mannie."

He called me Mannie when he was being sweet or really wanted me to do something.

The next day—the day of the game—ten-year-old Jon said, "Mama, do you think we could pray about the game tonight?"

I was surprised. I was usually the one who suggested to Jon and Jeremy that we pray about something. I put down the tomato I was slicing and went into the den. "Sure, Jon. I'd love to pray with you." I'd already been praying on my own about the game. Jon played shortstop and was good at his position. But tonight he had to pitch. It was only his second time pitching, and his team—the Yankees—were playing some really tough opponents.

After we prayed, I said, "Better go get those new cleats, Jon." Jeremy was playing too, but he didn't need new shoes. So Jon and I took off for the sporting-goods store, while Julie and Jen kept an eye on Jeremy.

Jon was unusually quiet in the store. After he tried the shoes on, he asked, "How much are they?" When the clerk told us, he looked quickly at me. I smiled reassuringly. Jon whispered to me, reminding me to ask for the ten percent discount that was allowed players on local teams. When we got home he laid the shoes out on his bed with his uniform. Then he told me, "They feel real good, Mama, and they're good-looking too. The best."

Back at home, Jon thought we should pray one more time just for good measure. We sat on the steps in the den. "Why don't we claim some Scripture?" I suggested. We'd done this before, so Jon understood.

"But what Scripture?" he asked.

I'd just discovered the Scripture in Habakkuk—I hadn't grown to love it yet, but I thought it fit the occasion. "Habakkuk three-nineteen. It's about hinds' feet."

"What kind of feet?" Jon sounded astonished.

I explained that hinds were deer with unusual feet, and that they could walk where other animals or even men couldn't walk. I told Jon, "When I have to do something really hard, something that could scare me, I think about that Scripture and believe that God can give me hinds' feet. That means that I can walk in places that would be impossible without His help. If we ask Him, He'll give you hinds' feet too."

He grinned and looked down at his feet as I read from the Bible. "'The Lord God is my strength, and He will make my feet like hinds' feet, and He will make me to walk upon mine high places.'"

"The pitcher's mound is a pretty high place," I added, hoping he understood.

"Yeah," he agreed, and we held hands to pray. Jon held mine so tightly that I almost drew it back. After I prayed, Jon prayed, "God, thank You for my new cleats. Help me do good tonight. Help Tim and Billy and the other boys. And make my feet just like . . . hinds' feet tonight."

From the beginning the other team looked great, especially their pitcher. Our fielding was way off. There were several doubtful calls from the umpires, and Jon walked quite a few players. Remembering how much the game meant to him, I kept praying, *Lord, give him those hinds' feet.*

Even though Jon's team was losing, I'd never been more proud of him. He stood erect, did his best, accepted the bad calls from the umpire. Several times when he pitched to a friend on the other team, he smiled, just as if he were pitching a no-hit game. I could tell from his enthusiasm that he never gave up hope of winning. When people shouted to him, telling him what he was doing wrong, he didn't get angry or frustrated. He kept his mind and heart on the game. I knew when he dropped his head before a pitch that he was praying.

Jon's team lost, sixteen to six.

After it was over, he shook hands with the players on the other team and said, "Good game." He didn't complain or blame anyone. He walked away from the field without murmuring. His new cleats were coated in red dust and I knew his heart was coated in disappointment.

Watching Jon walk toward the car, I thought about the years to come. The new cleats would be outgrown. But he had countless other shoes to walk in, through many difficult situations. Soon he'd fill the shoes of a teenager, then a husband—a father.

Will he remember back to the night that God gave him hinds' feet in baseball cleats? Will he remember that God can do it in any situation in life?

Despite everything that's happened since, I still like to think that he will, and someday, when he's a husband and a father, I hope Jon will tell his son about the night the Yankees lost their ballgame, and how he pitched wearing new cleats. I hope he'll tell his son how God gave him hinds' feet to walk calmly and surely right through the midst of defeat.

I was sitting at the foot of Jon's hospital bed remembering and holding on to one of his size twelve feet. "Mom, Mom. What's with holding on to my foot? You wanna let it go? You're about to cut off the circulation," he said with a laugh.

"Oh, sorry, Jon. I was thinking about something a long time ago."

"You were thinking about the time I pitched and lost and the story about hinds' feet in baseball cleats, weren't you?"

My mouth flew open.

"I know you pretty well, Mom."

I didn't say anything; I just smiled. But I knew Jon pretty well too. His time in the hospital was coming to a close. The surgeon was about to release him with detailed instructions for keeping his hand clean and changing the dressings at home—wherever home was—and a prescription for pain medicine.

Jon had no time or energy to worry about becoming addicted to the painkillers. His hand still looked pretty raw; we all prayed that the skin graft would take. Two fingers remained frozen, one in a strange position. It was very different from the large, square-shaped, freckle-covered hand it used to be. There were no freckles on the skin graft from his hip.

Marion, what a silly thing to think about. Be grateful he has a right hand. Never mind the freckles. Be grateful that he's left-handed.

I couldn't imagine Jon caring for his hand properly. Would

he go to the doctor for his scheduled visits? Would he keep the hand clean? Was there still a chance he'd lose it? But I was slowly learning to keep quiet about things I had no control over. I didn't even know for sure where he'd be living or how to get in touch with him.

A few months after Jon was released from the hospital, I got a call from Julie. "Mother, I happened to see Jon today. I didn't want to stare at his hand. We made small talk for a few minutes. But he still has a hand. He uses it too!"

"Oh, Julie, how wonderful! Does it work? Like a hand, I mean."

"Not all the fingers bend, and one is still crooked. The skin graft looks great, except that . . ."

"Except what?"

"There are no freckles on it," she said quietly.

I smiled. "I know. What does it look like?"

"Well, the best way I can describe it is to say that it's like a . . ." She spoke so softly I could hardly hear her. "It's sort of like a . . . a . . . Halloween hand."

"Oh."

"But it works, Mother!"

"That's marvelous. He kept his hand, Julie. God's so good."

"I've been searching the Internet," she added, knowing I had no computer and no desire to own one. "A lot of people die—very quickly—with what Jon had. Even big, strong men."

"They both made it, though, Julie. Jeremy will walk with a slight limp, and Jon's hand is . . . somewhat disfigured. But God saved them both again."

"We have to keep praying, Mother. It's not over yet."

"Yes, we'll pray and pray and then pray some more. For the decisions they've got to make. For their lives."

Thank You, Father, that Jon remembers that game, too, even after all this time. Thank You that I didn't forget to get him those cleats. Thank You that even though he's in such terrible danger now, I can sit on his hospital bed, hold his foot with the large freckle, and we can laugh together. Give him hinds' feet again to walk into victory and life. And give me hinds' feet, too, to walk with You wherever I must walk.

17 | TWINS—BUT, OH, HOW DIFFERENT

JON DID KNOW ME PRETTY WELL. Jeremy, too. Looking back—way back—I realize I didn't know them nearly as well as I should have. . . .

This Saturday was going to be long and lonely. Jerry, usually at home on weekends, would be gone all day because of a strike at Georgia Power. Jerry was in management, and he was working fourteen hours a day, plus Saturday. As a result, a kind of gloom had settled over our house. We *needed* Jerry.

Jon and Jeremy were about thirteen, and they missed their father terribly. He was a fun daddy, and he and the boys always did something special on Saturday—even if it was just a trip to Ace Hardware. Once when Jon had misbehaved and I had him write an essay for punishment, he entitled it "Saturdays Smell the Best." I cried reading it for the first time and nearly every other time I read it. His father understood him totally—Jeremy too. He never lost his temper with them, laughed a lot, knew how to listen and encourage them, and his face lit up when one of them entered the room.

On the other hand, there was me: Grim, determined, busy, on schedule—saying things like, "Sit up." "Take out the trash." "Do your homework." There were times when I felt like saying, "Don't have fun or enjoy life." Jerry was always the fun parent, and I the opposite. But I couldn't see that back then.

Both my sons stuck so close to Jerry on Saturdays that they

were like his shadows. I needed him too. Without him the day dragged by in slow motion. The boys cut the grass. Jon even got out the new hedge trimmer and used it. Jeremy picked the ripe tomatoes from the garden and brought them into the kitchen, a job that usually evoked a lot of conversation between Jeremy and his daddy. Then he polished his father's shoes. Long after they were gleaming brightly, he kept polishing them.

Finally it was dusk. Jon, Jeremy and I sat on the front porch looking hopefully down the darkening street. It was almost time for Jerry to come driving up. Tonight he wasn't eating at the company. He'd telephoned, asking us to wait for him. At a few minutes past nine we finally saw the car pull up in the driveway.

Like lightning, Jon leaped over two steps and galloped to meet him. He called out to Jerry as he ran, loudly relating the events of the day. Suddenly I felt uneasy about Jeremy. He had his head down on his folded arms. As Jon and Jerry came closer, Jeremy didn't lift his head. Jerry looked down at him and then at me with a puzzled look. I didn't understand Jeremy's behavior. Jerry touched Jeremy's red hair and said, "Hey, Buddy." He didn't ask as I would have, "Why are you so quiet?"

Jeremy looked up. It was obvious that he was fighting hard to keep back the tears. We were all surprised. Jon even slowed down his rapid-fire conversation and pretended to study a fly on the screen.

"Come on in, Jon, and help me get supper on the table," I said. He came without his usual protest. We left Jeremy and his daddy on the front steps.

The minutes ticked by. Supper was ready, but I hesitated to call them in. Instead, I peeked out the living room window. Jeremy now stood on a step above his father so that he was Jerry's height. They stood motionless, holding on to each other. Jeremy's head was on his father's shoulder, and his arms were wound tightly around his neck. They didn't seem to be talking. I knew in Jerry's place I would have asked countless questions. I also knew that he hadn't asked even one.

When finally they came in, Jeremy's eyes were red from crying. We sat down in unusual silence. Julie and Jennifer mostly looked at their food and refrained from asking questions. I was surprised when Jerry asked Jeremy to ask the blessing. I wasn't certain he could get through a prayer. His voice cracked, and he sniffed several times. But he managed. "Thank You, God, for this food. Thank You that Daddy is here to eat with us tonight. We pray for a good church service tomorrow. Please let the strike be over soon. Amen."

Later that night I stuck my head in each boy's room. Jon was already asleep. But Jeremy was lying on his back looking out his window. I could see his face in the soft moonlight. "'Night, Jeremy."

"'Night, Mama."

I hesitated, moving closer. "Jeremy, was anything wrong today? I mean . . ."

He didn't answer right away, still looking out at the stars. Finally he said, "I missed Daddy a lot today. A lot more than I thought I would. I got to thinking . . . Suppose he wasn't ever coming home again? Suppose every day would be like today? Then when I saw Daddy drive up, I was so glad to see him that I . . . couldn't say anything. I just sat there. But he's a good daddy. He understood, ya know. He really understood."

I kissed him and left him looking out the window at the heavens and thinking his thoughts.

When I came back into our bedroom, Jerry was already asleep. I sat for a moment on the edge of the bed, going over the day in my mind. And suddenly I realized that just because people don't talk a lot, like I do, doesn't mean they aren't communicating.

I was so grateful that Jerry understood them both and hadn't asked Jeremy, "What's wrong, son? Why are you so quiet?"

Jon and Jeremy were totally different. The nurse who showed them to me when they were born had been right: They were just brothers that got born at the same time. They were never going to be any more alike than Jerry and I were alike.

When Jerry first went to the hospital about a year later and the doctors couldn't discover his problem, Jon was mostly silent— but I knew he was thinking, hoping, praying.

Jeremy, on the other hand had volunteered, "Mom, I'll quit school and go to work if daddy can't work any more." He'd said it matter-of-factly.

I heard myself say, "Oh, honey, he's going to be fine—you'll see!"

Even then I didn't believe my own words.

And after Jerry's unsuccessful surgery for the cancer, it had been Jeremy who brought his daddy a strange gift. I had no idea he'd bought it. Jerry had unwrapped it slowly, as if it were Christmas morning, and exclaimed, "Wow, Jeremy—great!"

It was a small box of tools. Written on the box was: *The Master's Tools.*

I prayed silently standing there with Jon and Jeremy, Julie and Jennifer, *Oh, Lord, please use Jerry in some wonderful way as a tool of Yours. Please let him live and be Your tool.*

Father, thank You for the memories Jon and Jeremy have of their father. I want to learn to communicate without talking nonstop; Jerry and Jon and Jeremy did it just by looking into each other's eyes. Let me learn that love can be quick and quiet and simple.

18 | THE CONVERSATION

A FEW MONTHS AFTER his father's death, Jon said something I'll never forget. We were having some difficult times. Both Jon and Jeremy were exhibiting signs of rebellion. In retrospect, I wish I'd made them deal openly with their grief. I grieved so hard caring for Jerry the ten months before he died, that a big chunk of my grief had been worked through. But my sons, who'd just turned fifteen, had all their emotions pent up inside.

There were some nice times in between the arguments and shouting and my grilling them about where they'd been.

I was lying on my bed studying the ceiling late one Friday afternoon when Jon came and sat down by me. I figured he wanted something—permission to do something that he knew I wouldn't want him to do. He said, "Mom, we were never very close when Daddy was alive. It's sort of fun getting to know you now. Sort of."

I was startled and for a moment couldn't respond. I'd been seeing things in him that I admired lately. He never complained, almost never lost his temper. Both his strength and weakness was his phlegmatic temperament. He wasn't highly motivated, except about a few things, like eating and playing tennis.

I had been lying there that June afternoon thinking: *You're going to be alone tonight, and lonely. You are dreading it, aren't you? All the children have plans. . . .*

Outside, lawn mowers were humming. Husbands who'd gotten home early enough from work were taking advantage of the long days, getting a head start on the lawns. *If Jerry were here, he'd be cutting the grass. But he's not. You are alone. Alone!* At least our yard looked great. Jeremy had assumed the responsibility of caring for it. He did a magnificent job. It never needed cutting now.

That's what I'd been thinking when Jon sat down by me. Then he stretched out on the bed in his daddy's place, a place I avoided looking at usually. Nag that I was, I said, "You're going to be late for your party." I had nagged Jerry about time too.

"It's okay," he said with a laugh. "Nobody wants to be early for a party. It's nerdy." His voice was different: gentle, soft. He hugged the pillow that had been his father's and stared at the ceiling with me as though we were watching an overhead television. I recognized his mood; he was that much like his father.

"You have something on your mind, Jon. Just say it."

"Naw, Mom. Nothing. Just not ready to take my shower."

"Jon, what is it?" My voice was edged with irritation. Why couldn't I have been patient, smiling—enjoying him?

"It's nothing, Mom," he said, still using that gentle voice. Minutes passed. He struggled with unspoken words; I could almost feel them sitting there deep inside him. Finally, he said, "Mom, you want me to stay home tonight?"

His words hit me unexpectedly, like sweet syrup running all over me. I didn't want him to miss the party—not this one. It was an okay one. I guess I just wanted him to offer to stay with me. I didn't even know I needed to hear those words until he said them.

"Oh no, Jon. I want you to go."

"You didn't eat supper, Mom. When will you eat?"

"I'm not hungry. You know food's no big deal with me."

I could go somewhere with you and talk to you while you eat. I'll have food at the party . . . if I go."

"Thanks, Jon. Really, I'm not hungry."

More silence, then he said, "I've been thinking about some of the things you said when you came to our school."

I'd done a little teaching on creative writing at his and Jeremy's school at the teacher's invitation. Jon had begged me not to come. "You'll say something weird," he'd insisted.

"I'm coming, Jon. I hope you live through it. I want to do this with the students." I hadn't thought he'd listened to a word I said. He'd looked at his feet most of the time I was there.

Jon said without warning, "I could probably write about when Daddy died."

I was stunned. Suddenly I sat up on the bed, behaving like a teacher: "What did your learn from this experience? What was your turning point? Was there an unlikely character who helped you?"

"I—I—guess you're the unlikely character, Mom."

"Me! I didn't think you approved of anything I did. You even said I seemed to have too much joy after your daddy died."

"I know. But now that I think about it, you didn't fall apart or anything. Didn't scream. Didn't even cry much. You just smiled a sad smile and kept on going. You were very efficient with all the plans and all. I like efficiency."

"Oh, Jon. I have to tell you something. I haven't told a soul, but I need to talk about it. I can now. Before I finally let go of Daddy and decided to trust God as never before, I thought about killing myself. I'd done so many things wrong as a wife. When

Daddy got sick, I suddenly learned what was important, and then he was going to be gone—just when I'd gotten it all together. It seemed so totally unfair."

It was perhaps the longest and certainly the deepest conversation of our lives. Jon hated what I called "meaningful conversation." His daddy had too—until that last year. Then we talked for hours. "Mom," Jon asked, looking strange, "how were you going to kill yourself?" We were both lying down again, staring at the ceiling with the nice noise that lawnmowers make in the background. The late afternoon sun cast shadows in my bedroom, and I was talking to my son.

"I thought about going around that curve on the expressway too fast. You know, the one where the students from Emory do mountain climbing."

"But Mom, there's no cliff down where the road is. You just would have gone into the grass. Probably gotten stuck. You wouldn't even have hurt yourself."

I sat up on my elbow. "Really?"

Jon started to laugh, slowly at first, then faster, like a train gaining speed. He had his father's dry humor. He curled up in a ball, holding onto the pillow and laughing. I started to laugh too.

He was laughing so hard, his eyes were squeezed shut and his voice high pitched. "Oh, Mom, you would have messed that up good—like only you can do. Remember the time you cleaned Daddy's paintbrush by putting it in the gas tank in the lawn mower?"

We laughed together and made little squeaking noises rolling around on the bed until our stomachs hurt and tears rolled into my ears. Finally we became quiet. Jon asked, "What will you do when we're all gone from here?"

I tried to appear casual. His question caught me off guard. "I don't know. It's not my problem. I belong to God. He'll have to figure that one out."

"Would you ever get married again?" The question was totally unexpected. But so was this entire conversation and the marvelous laughter.

"If that's God's plan for my life. I'd like to love someone again."

Still looking at the ceiling and hugging a pillow, he said, "I think that would be a good idea, Mom. But you know," he laughed softly as though he didn't really want to get started all over again, "it would have to be someone that was . . . a nut like you. I mean, you do weird stuff. And he'd have to be a Jesus freak."

I laughed again. "I know, Jon. Just an average somebody wouldn't work. I'll always do weird stuff, and Jesus will always be number one."

We both continued looking up at the ceiling, silently now. And then, "Mom, you're crying! You *never* cry. You didn't even cry at Daddy's funeral."

I couldn't explain. I hadn't expected tears. Maybe my tear ducts got opened up laughing. These were sweet, grateful tears—for Jon's concern and the wonderful conversation and the laughter—his love and gentleness.

As I wiped my tears on the pillowcase, he said, "I really don't care about the party. I'm staying home tonight."

Enough tears. I got up. "No. You're going. I'm fine, better than you can imagine. Finish getting ready." When he came back to the bedroom, all dressed and smelling good, I saw him looking at my red-rimmed eyes. "I know, Jon. You can tell I've been crying. I'll wear dark glasses driving you to the party."

At his friend's house I let him out. "Have a good time."

Why hadn't we had more fun times like this—more conversations?

I love you, Jon.

Father, sometimes Jon amazes me. I needed to have that conversation with someone. Who would have thought it would be Jon? I know I talk too much. Help me learn to listen.

PART FIVE

"THOUGH THE FLOCK
SHOULD BE CUT OFF
FROM THE FOLD..."

19 | FITTING IN

FOR THE FIRST WEEKS Jeremy was at Mulberry Grove Assisted Living, he refused to leave his room. He was sullen and depressed; he lay in his bed and stared at the ceiling with the curtains closed and the lights off. With his broken right hip and left leg, he needed help moving about or getting to the bathroom, but he didn't want to ask for it. Some of the aides there were girls his age.

I visited Jeremy several times a day. I offered to take him outside or out to the lobby, but he didn't want to get into his wheelchair. I exhausted myself day after day trying to get him to respond, smile, ask for something, or just look me in the eye. He responded better to Gene. Gene would go into Jeremy's room, turn on a ballgame, and settle down quietly, and after awhile Jeremy would say something like, "Do you think the Braves will win, Gene?"

One day I ran into Julie at the entrance to Mulberry Grove. "What do you think we'll find today?" I asked, exasperated.

"Whatever it is," Julie said, "why don't you just play it cool and not respond to his behavior. Don't try so hard. It's not working."

We found Jeremy in bed in his dark room. He had refused breakfast and a bath. "Hi, Germany," Julie sang out. It was the name he'd been called in first grade because not many boys were named Jeremy back in 1974, when he and Jon were six. There was just enough light in the room for Julie and me to see a quick flash of a smile cross his face. He made a huge effort and got the grim look back again.

"You want company?" Julie asked again, picking up some clothing from the floor.

We both watched for any sign of an answer. He shrugged his shoulders in bed, his eyes closed.

"We don't want to bother you. We'll come back later. Bye." She reached and grabbed my arm and pulled me toward the door.

"You don't have to go," he said quickly.

Julie had always assumed responsibility for him. On the day we brought the twins home from the hospital, I'd handed Jeremy to eight-year-old Julie and Jon to six-year-old Jennifer as they sat on the sofa, their little legs sticking straight out, hands washed and all ready for their little brothers. Jeremy looked enough like Julie to be hers—both had deep, wavy red hair. Jon's hair was more of a strawberry blond and Jennifer's was a reddish-auburn.

I was tremendously encouraged that he wanted us to stay. At least he wanted Julie to stay—I hung around, remembering not to talk too much.

It took weeks, but at last he got up the nerve to come out of his room, encouraged by Bobby, the elderly man across the hall. Bobby had rolled his chair into Jeremy's room the day we moved him in. He was loud, asked too many questions, gave us information we didn't want, and seemed to plant himself there while we were trying to get Jeremy settled.

"Hi, there, Germany," he said. He was tall, even in his wheelchair, and lean, with gray thinning hair and lively, humorous eyes. "His name's Jeremy, J-e-r-e-m-y," I said sternly. I'd never liked that nickname.

"Germany, we're neighbors and I want us to be friends. I'll be around to help you out. Watch out for the girls here. Good looking young thing like you; they'll be all over you like monkeys on a june bug." Bobby laughed. Because he was hard of hearing, he talked much too loudly.

I looked at Bobby with my meanest expression, but he ignored me. He patted Jeremy's left foot and I hollered, "Be careful—that leg's broken."

"Germany's tough. I can tell," Bobby said. "Your mama needs to stop babying you," he said to Jeremy. Then he turned to me. "Why don't you leave him be?" Bobby snarled.

"Why don't you just leave our room?" I said, about ready to shove his chair out into the hall.

"You don't scare me none, Mama," Bobby said with a laugh. "See this cane? I pack a mean wallop." He held up the wooden walking stick he carried across his lap.

I picked up Jeremy's walker. "Want to fight?" I said. Anger boiled inside me because of Jeremy's circumstances, my weariness, and my fear of what the future held for him. My rage surprised me, but I made no effort to control it.

"I like your mama, Germany. She's spunky," Bobby said. He put his cane back across his lap. "I'm leaving now. See ya. Hey, do you play checkers? Or watch the Braves?"

"I do both," Jeremy said, a slow smile playing around his mouth. "Thanks, Bobby, for coming by. See you."

After a while, when any of us arrived to visit Jeremy, we'd find him with Bobby, playing checkers or watching the ballgame in Bobby's room, where the television reception was better than in Jeremy's room. They ate at the same table too. Every day Bobby gave Jeremy his dessert. So did a lot of the others. And the girls waiting the tables often brought Jeremy two meals. His weight went from a scant hundred and fifty to slightly over two hundred pounds. He was huge; we had to buy him new clothes.

As Jeremy's recovery progressed, I'd pick him up in Gene's station wagon and bring him out to our house for a meal. It wasn't long after we'd finished eating that Jeremy would say, "Well, I better be going. Bobby and I are watching the ballgame tonight. He'll be expecting me."

One day we checked Jeremy out to take him to the orthopedist for his regular visit. Bobby was sitting in the lobby, pretending to try to get some of the women sitting there to hug him. 'Where ya taking Germany?" he bellowed at me.

"Hi, Bobby," I said. I smiled; I couldn't help but smile. I'd come to adore Bobby. I'd spent so much time in assisted-living facilities and nursing homes with my mother and Jerry's parents that anyone with spunk seemed okay in my book. Besides, he was Jeremy's best friend. "We're just taking him for a regular checkup."

"You gonna bring him back, ain't ya?"

"What if I don't?" I teased.

"Then I'll come looking for ya. You bring him back, hear?"

"Bobby, I'll be back in a couple of hours," Jeremy said gently. Bobby beamed. "Okay boy. I'll be waiting on ya."

One day Jeremy phoned me at home and said, "Tomorrow's Bobby's birthday."

"Oh, Jeremy, I'll fix him a birthday basket, okay?"

"Sure, he'll like that, Mom. Thanks."

I got a huge basket and filled it with goodies—cookies and candy that I knew he liked, Cokes, reading material, handkerchiefs, nuts—things I'd seen in his room. I fixed a card and signed it, "Love from Jeremy, Gene, and Marion."

Amazingly Bobby and I had the same birthday—July 8. He got a big kick out of that. And he told everyone about his birthday basket.

Bobby had a cat at home, and every other day he drove his ancient car the few blocks to his home to feed the cat. "He really loves that cat, Mom," Jeremy explained. Love of cats was enough to keep the three of us close—but more and more beneath Bobby's rough exterior, I got glimpses of a gentle, kind, soft-hearted man. Even so, he delighted in making scenes, angering the little old ladies and even the management of Mulberry Grove.

He loved to threaten people with his stick, and naturally this scared older folks, and they drew back or reported him. I found an old wooden walking stick of my stepfather's at our house and took it with me on a visit.

When Bobby railed at me with his stick up in the air, I threw mine up too, sort of like we were sword-fighting. We clattered our sticks together loudly and shouted at each other. By now I was totally comfortable with whatever Bobby did. Jeremy laughed and said, "Watch out, Bobby. She's really angry!" Bobby was sent to his room by the management, and I made an effort not to cane fight with him in the lobby.

By now Jeremy was spending less and less time in his room and was walking slowly with a walker. He fit in at Mulberry Grove—he was everyone's grandson and Bobby's good buddy; it was wonderful to see them laughing together. He had grown to love the place. And belonging gave him a certain quiet joy and contentment.

Father, when I think I have You all figured out, You show me that You are larger and grander than I imagined. You put Jeremy and Bobby Harris together for Your purposes. Help me remember that You often select the most unlikely people to carry out Your plans.

THE JOY OF | 20
BELONGING |

THE JOY OF BELONGING. As I drove home from visiting Jeremy one day at Mulberry, that phrase played around in my head like an old tune. Just as I drove up in our driveway, a long-ago memory eased itself into my mind. . . .

It had been Jon who told me about the Farmers, our neighbors in the new subdivision we'd moved into when the boys were about six. We lived in a typical suburban home, but the Farmers' house was an old, unpainted farmhouse with a working outhouse behind it. Jon had liked Mr. Farmer right away; I'd often seen him at the fence, talking to the friendly-looking man in overalls.

Jon had told me that Mr. and Mrs. Farmer had lived there for a very long time. They had raised children there, and now they were alone. One day Mr. Farmer knocked on our back door. Jon got to the door before I did and looked up, beaming at his new friend.

"Hi, Mr. Farmer," I said. "I'm Jon's mother, Marion. Come in, won't you?"

"No, ma'am," he said matter-of-factly. "Me and the missus wanted to welcome you all. We're making music this Saturday night on our front porch. Hope you'll come and bring the young 'uns. Good day, ma'am."

Mr. Farmer was middle aged, maybe older. I was a young thing then, and when I told Jerry about Mr. Farmer's visit, he beamed. "Well, we *must* go." We had a fine time watching Mr. Farmer and his friends "make music" on the old wooden front porch. They played a harmonica, a banjo and a guitar, and everyone sang. Even Jerry and the children and I joined in. I had a great time singing "I'll Fly Away."

Mr. Farmer brought us vegetables from his garden, and we became friends. Then one day I was standing at the sink doing dishes when I saw a thin white cat on the back porch of Mr. Farmer's house. I have this need to rescue stray cats. *Don't get involved, Marion,* I told myself sternly.

A battle began inside me—a very familiar one. Part of me wanted desperately to turn away and never look at the starving cat again. Jerry had warned me time and time again that I'd end up as a little old lady in tennis shoes rescuing every stray cat I found and bringing them all home. He even showed me a picture of a woman like that in the paper. I loved her. *God bless her!*

I wiped my hands on my apron, grabbed a pack of cat food and headed for the old house. The cat darted beneath the porch as I approached. The house sat on concrete blocks; I crawled part of the way under it and called, "Here, Kitty." Two slanted bright eyes gleamed at me. I could almost feel the cat's hunger, but it wouldn't come to me, so I left the food underneath the house.

Mr. Farmer had told Jerry that stray cats hung around his house, but none were his. He and Mrs. Farmer only had an older, much loved dog.

For several months I fed the cat this way. Then I noticed another cat with her—a male, solid white, obviously a grown son still with his mother. Soon I was feeding both of them. I never met up with either of the Farmers during my missions.

One day while I fed them, the mama cat came cautiously toward me and rubbed her face against my hand for a brief moment; then fear sprang into her eyes and she darted away. But after that she met me at the fence at five each day. The other cat would scamper away and hide in the bushes waiting for me to leave.

I always talked to them as I put out their food, calling them by the names I'd given them, Mama and Brother. One day as Mama rubbed slowly against my leg with eyes almost shut in contentment, she purred for the first time. My hand didn't reach out, not yet, but my heart did. After that she often rubbed against me and allowed me to stroke her, even before she touched the food. Brother, reluctant and stiff-necked, allowed me to touch him only occasionally, but he always endured my affection, never received it.

The cats grew fat. As I sat at my desk one day, I saw Mama Kitty on my patio. She had never come into my yard before. My own cats would never permit it, and yet here she was. "Good for you, Mama," I said to myself. Suddenly, she leaped into the air, and I thought for a moment that she might be choking. Then she seemed to be chasing something rapidly across the patio. Mama Kitty was playing for perhaps the first time in her life. I watched her toss an acorn into the air and leap up after it. Then my own cats came lurking toward the patio door to try to hiss this strange cat away from the inside. Brave Mama only looked at them, and continued playing with the acorn in the sunshine. Brother sat on the fence waiting for supper.

That summer Mama Kitty had kittens. By watching her I figured that she'd had them in the attic of the Farmers' old house. One day when the Farmers had gone to visit their daughter, she came to my backdoor to get me. I went with her, followed her up some old stairs on the outside of the house, and crawled somewhat reluctantly into the dark attic. I tried to ignore the spiders, dust, heat, and rattling sounds that I suspected were mice. Finally, I located the three tiny kittens. Brother stood guard over them. He backed up, and I gathered the tiny babies into my hand.

I brought them down and fixed a box for them out in an old shed behind the Farmers' house. Mama Kitty didn't seem too happy about my moving her kittens, but she allowed them to stay for a while anyway.

I heard some barking during the night and the next day, the kittens weren't where I'd put them. I just knew she'd moved them back into the hot attic. Reluctantly, I knocked on the door and explained to the Farmers about the cat. They listened patiently to my long, drawn-out, somewhat confused story. When they understood that I wanted to go up to their attic, they gave me permission right away. Mr. Farmer even gave me his flashlight.

Once in the attic, I discovered Mama Kitty had moved the kittens to a new spot. I had no idea where, and I couldn't find them.

I went back three times, apologizing each time for being a bother, but I was still unable to find the kittens. I'd stand at the kitchen sink and look out at the old house with its tin roof. I could see the heat rising off of it—the temperature was in the upper nineties. How long could the kittens survive?

I had nagged Jerry to do something, cried, and prayed. Jeremy had offered to help me rescue them. "I don't know where they are, son," I told him.

"God knows," he'd replied. "He can show you."

The next morning before I even opened my eyes, I prayed one more time, "Lord, please get those kittens out of the attic. I don't think I have any more faith. But Jeremy does. Please help us. Don't let the kittens die."

I hopped out of bed and ran to the back door, half expecting to see the kittens sitting on the back step. Of course, they weren't. No sign of Mama, or Brother either. It was going to be another hot day.

"Go look again, Mama," Jeremy begged. "I'll stay here and pray."

That's all it took for me to go and knock on the Farmers' door—again.

Without much enthusiasm, Mrs. Farmer said that I could go to the attic. As soon as I got up there, I heard the meowing. "I'm coming. I'm coming," I called out joyfully. *Keep praying, Jeremy.*

The next moment I couldn't figure out what had happened. I seemed to be falling. Plaster broke loose. I wasn't in the dark, hot attic anymore, but dangling into the kitchen. Most of me, that is. I'd forgotten to stay on the rafters and crashed through the Farmers' kitchen ceiling over the breakfast table where they were eating. I tried to pull myself up, but I just kept breaking off more and more plaster that joined my shoes on the table below.

Thoroughly shaken, I finally climbed back down out of the attic. In the kitchen, my new neighbors and I observed the damage. I grabbed a broom and began sweeping. More plaster fell onto us and we coughed in the dust. I apologized over and over, babbling that we would have the ceiling fixed. We all had white plaster in our hair. "I'll bring my husband over to talk to y'all," I assured the startled but patient-looking couple. On top of everything else, I didn't have the kittens. When I'd started falling, I'd quickly put the three kittens down safely.

That night at supper I explained what had happened to Jerry

and the children. They all stared at me silently, sort of like the Farmers had. I was close to tears, partly because of the plight of the kittens and partly because of my own stupidity.

Jerry said, "I want you to go back tomorrow and speak to Mr. Farmer. Tell him we'll have the damage repaired. And promise him that you'll never go into their attic again."

I nodded. Jerry said in a softer voice, "Want me to go with you?"

I shook my head.

I arrived the next day during a meal. The couple's children were eating with them. They all stared at me as they continued eating. I was introduced as "That woman who goes up in the attic all the time and fell through yesterday." I smiled at all of them, or tried to. Mr. Farmer stood up and said solemnly, "Maw, get my gun." For one horrible moment, my heart froze. Then he broke into a little-boy grin and continued, "Forget it. I'm a carpenter, and the ceiling needed repairing, anyway."

I smiled back at him and added, "My husband wanted me to tell you that I'd never go up in your attic again—not ever."

"Okay," he said with a grin. I thought I heard Mrs. Farmer sigh.

The next day was Sunday. That afternoon we were all sitting in the living room reading the paper. Only I wasn't reading; I was praying behind my section of paper. I just couldn't forget about those kittens. The more I prayed, the more I thought I actually heard the kittens mewing!

Then the doorbell rang, and we all ran for it. I got there first, and there stood Mr. Farmer, cobwebs in his hair, dust on his overalls, and the little-boy grin on his lean, suntanned face. We all looked down, and there, cradled in his huge hands, were the kittens. "Lady, you won't have to look for 'em anymore. I found 'em for you."

Mama Kitty was a safe distance behind him meowing, and out back on the fence sat Brother, waiting for his five o'clock feeding.

I put the kittens in our shed in the carport, and Mama Kitty let them stay. We found loving homes for all of them. I had Mama Kitty spayed. She started coming right up to the back door and meowing and purring when she was hungry. After a while she'd even come inside, despite my own cat's hissing and generally unkind attitude. On cold nights she slept curled up in one of our kitchen chairs. She knew the joy of belonging.

Oh, Father, Mr. Farmer was such a gentle, kind, genuine man. Jon sure knew how to pick 'em. Thank You that he forgave me for falling through the ceiling. Thank You for hearing my prayers, even when they're for something as small as those three kittens.

21 | LOOKING OUT MY KITCHEN WINDOW

THE FARMERS AND JERRY AND I and even our children became good friends through the years. I always enjoyed doing dishes because I got to look out my kitchen window and see the rugged old house, surrounded by the modern brick homes of our subdivision and often get a glimpse of our neighbors. Something about them fascinated and comforted me.

I loved to watch them take the clothes off the line at the end of the day. It never failed to make me smile, no matter how hard my day had been.

In the summertime, Mr. Farmer left their garden to help his wife. In the winter, he stuck his ax in an old stump and joined her to take down the clothes, although I never saw her ask for help. They seemed to share a special joy in doing the job together. Many evenings as I watched out my kitchen window, the sun formed a red backdrop in our north Georgia sky and the Farmers appeared against it as small, reaching silhouettes. I envied them.

Even though I'd enjoyed the smell of freshly hung-out sheets, I'd dreaded taking them in. I never hung out clothes anymore; I just threw them in the dryer. But after watching the Farmers, I considered hanging out my wash again and asking Jerry to help me take it in. I decided, however, that it wouldn't work for us. It was their thing—something they'd done together for years without the need for words.

There were times, late on a summer afternoon after the clothes had been taken in, when the Farmers sat on their front porch swing and watched the cars whiz by their house. As Jerry and I sat on our new redwood furniture, enjoying our patio, I tried to assure myself that we were much like the Farmers.

Mr. Farmer still invited us over to make music on the front porch. One day, when the power went off during an ice storm, he invited the six of us to stay with them. "We have a wood-burning stove, and it's nice and warm at our house. Bring the children and come on over," he urged. I was astonished: Even I didn't want to be shut up with the twins during an ice storm. We'd already accepted another invitation, but I wished we could have spent some time with them.

Mr. Farmer brought us beautiful vegetables straight from his garden. Looking out my kitchen window, I'd see him coming. I liked the way he looked in overalls. Some people don't look comfortable in them, and others look sloppy. But Mr. Farmer appeared professional.

The Farmers didn't have a lot of the things that most of us think of as necessities, like an indoor bathroom or a car, but I never thought so much about what they didn't have as about what they *did* have. I finally decided why I envied them: They were contented people.

One day Mr. Farmer spoke to me over the back fence. "Y'all come over some evening. We'll listen to the radio, or I'll play my new little organ for you." We talked often of going over to visit the Farmers, but somehow, with all the children's activities—piano practice, sports, cheerleading—we never got around to it.

Then one Sunday I went over to check on our boys, who had climbed the fence to play with some of the Farmers' twenty-six grandchildren. The sun's rays slanted across their long back porch. A cat slept in an upholstered chair, and as I walked up the plank steps, a myriad of cats' eyes shining in the darkness under the house looked back at me. At least there were no kittens now.

Mr. Farmer was already on his feet, offering me a chair. As I sat down, Mrs. Farmer closed the Sears catalog they'd been reading together. He began talking, and she smiled and nodded, listening intently to him. It was a rather cold day, but I felt warm and secure as I sat there.

Mr. Farmer talked about the kind of winter we were likely to have and recalled some of the severe weather he'd experienced when he was a little boy. "My daddy said, 'Run, son! Run to the school and tell them a tornado's coming.' I ran fast as I could and just beat the tornado. None of them was hurt, but lots of other folks was."

He motioned to a big red dog that lay with his eyes closed in the sun on the porch. "I found that dog with his throat slit. Brought him home and sewed it up, and he follows me everywhere I go. He's a good dog." Without opening his eyes, the dog flopped his long tail up and down.

A couple of weeks later, I saw the dog struck and killed by a car. I went to the Farmers' house to tell them. Even before she let the hurt sink in, Mrs. Farmer thanked me for coming and offered me some coffee.

It was just a few days before Thanksgiving when one of their children discovered Mrs. Farmer dead on the kitchen floor. I didn't hear about it until late that night, and I went over early the next morning. Heavy frost covered the ground. Sunlight shone from the tin roof, but the house looked still and cold. I went up the back steps and across the long porch, and knocked gently on the weather-beaten door. Instantly Mr. Farmer opened it.

"Come in, Mrs. West. How are you? Come sit here by the stove. Cold, isn't it?" He resumed his task of drying the dishes and scrubbed the sink long after it was clean. I sat by the stove watching him, not sure whether to take off my coat or not.

Then he began talking, and I slid out of my coat and listened. The little dog he'd found after the big one got killed came into the kitchen. His tiny feet made scratching sounds as he scooted across the linoleum. He sniffed me, then jumped into Mr. Farmer's lap as he took a seat in a rocking chair. "He's still looking for Mama," Mr. Farmer explained. "It'll take him a while to understand."

Several times I reached for my coat and said that I needed to go, but he insisted, "You needn't hurry." I sensed he meant it, so I stayed nearly two hours, listening.

I was so comfortable with him that I didn't even look away when he spit his tobacco juice into a coffee can. His grandchildren came in and drank from the kitchen faucet, using the dipper that hung within their reach. I watched, thinking what a practical idea that was. He kept talking, almost as though he were unaware of them and their loudness.

I don't know why, but Mr. Farmer wore little round sunglasses all the time. I thought they made him look distinguished. In fact, I'd never seen him without them. But while he was talking he took them off suddenly, just for a moment. His eyes were a clear, penetrating blue. But the raw grief in them shocked me so that I nearly gasped out loud.

He put the glasses back on matter-of-factly and laughed, remembering another funny story. I relaxed again.

He told me of his boyhood days and of the times after he and Mrs. Farmer were married. "I worked for eleven dollars a week," he said with a chuckle, "and I didn't know tomatoes came in a can till I was seventeen years old." Without complaining, he recounted the hard times and the raising of seven children. He remembered the year his entire crop failed. Then he said in a softer voice, "Me and Mama used to love to sit by the fire and listen to it crackle. You ever listened to a fire? I left her sitting by the fire yesterday. She was fine."

I went back several times during the next days, taking food and inquiring about funeral arrangements. Each time he thanked me for coming with such sincerity that I felt embarrassed. It was the way he said, "We sure do appreciate the food. Thank you. Thank you for coming, Mrs. West."

I told Mr. Farmer what a beautiful dress they'd selected for Mrs. Farmer. I don't think I'll ever forget it: baby blue, long-sleeved, with a Peter Pan collar, a soft material.

He smiled, "The man at the store kept bringing out lacy, frilly dresses. And I kept telling him no, that she liked plain things. Never did like nothing fancy. I knew the minute I saw the blue dress."

"She would have loved it, Mr. Farmer."

He nodded for a long time.

Late in the afternoon a few weeks later I couldn't find Jon. I called him and searched the street. No one had seen him, and I began to be concerned. Then looking out my kitchen window, I saw him running across Mr. Farmer's long back porch, hopping down the steps, and hurrying to the fence. He scrambled over it and was nearly out of breath by the time he came through the kitchen door.

"I've been worried about you," I said in a stern voice even before he shut the back door.

"Sorry, Mama," he gasped. "I saw it was getting dark and

came home. I've been over to Mr. Farmer's. He invited me in, and I thought it might hurt his feelings if I didn't go. We've been talking." He grinned proudly, as only an excited six-year-old can.

"About what?" I asked, not quite ready to let go of my anger.

"Oh, lots of things, Mama. Mr. Farmer likes to talk to me. We talk about the weather and high prices and when he was a little boy like me, and lots of good stuff. We played a game too."

My anger melted and I heard my voice soften. "I'm glad you went, Jon, but next time, tell me, okay?"

"Okay, Mama. I'm going back soon. Mr. Farmer really likes me. He's real nice, ain't he?"

I didn't even correct his English; I just agreed. "Yes, Jon. He's one of the nicest people I've ever known."

I looked out the window as I spoke and saw Mr. Farmer coming out his back door. He walked to the clothesline with the familiar basket and began taking down the clothes, folding them carefully. His little dog, right at his feet, watched. After he'd gathered the clothes, he walked slowly but with determination back to the house. The sky was now a deep red.

He held the door open for the little dog, and they went inside. The light came on in his kitchen, and smoke poured out of the chimney. I stood looking out my kitchen window and cried.

Father, You have a way of putting me near people You want me to learn from. I want to be gentle and brave and accepting like Mr. Farmer is. Give me courage and keep me from self-pity.

22 | REMEMBERING

MR. FARMER DIED UNEXPECTEDLY six months after Mrs. Farmer. The day after his funeral was blustery and cold, but the sun was out. I'd done the wash, and when I pulled the sheets and other things from the washing machine, I couldn't get myself to put them in the dryer. I stood there for a few minutes arguing silently with myself. Finally, I put the clothes in the yellow plastic clothes basket with the broken handle and trudged out back. I had to go back inside to find some clothespins.

I stretched the sheets out smoothly, trying not to see the Farmers at their clothesline in my mind. Somehow it helped to hang out my wash.

Later that afternoon I looked through closets and in various stacks around the house until I found a Sears catalog. Instead of watching television, I thumbed through the huge, battered old book. I was still reading it when the children came in from school. That's what the Farmers had said—"reading it." Julie, Jennifer, Jon and Jeremy came running down to the den and sat down around me. We turned the pages slowly. Someone had something to say about an item on practically every page.

"Hey, that's what I want for Christmas!" Jeremy said, pointing to a cowboy outfit.

"Me too," Jon echoed.

We looked at girls' clothing and dolls, and men's things, tools, and lawn equipment for Jerry. And they even found some cooking things they thought I'd like. It was like magic: no fussing or "Do your homework, now!" or "Can I go down to Bryan's, Mama?" or "Why can't we have what I want for supper?" or "It's his turn to take out the trash"; just me, sitting there with my four children and two cats, talking softly, laughing some, all of us touching.

When I washed the lunch dishes at the kitchen sink that day, I tried to look down at the dishes and concentrate on them, but finally I looked up and out to the old house standing empty now. And the memories floated back over the fence, across my backyard, and through the kitchen window, right into my heart. And I missed the Farmers and began my grieving there at the kitchen sink.

When I went out to take in the clothes late that afternoon, I didn't throw them in the basket haphazardly as I always had. I folded the sheets and towels carefully into neat squares and smelled the sweet sunshine clinging stubbornly to them.

That night the boys had a basketball game. Jerry hurried through supper to get them there early and then take the girls to their activities. I begged off and stayed home alone. The house was so quiet, it felt almost as if it wasn't mine. After cleaning up the kitchen, I went down into the den and reached for the *TV Guide*. I put it back on the table unopened.

I didn't know a lot about making a fire, but I'd watched Jerry enough so that I thought I could get one going. So I went outside and brought in some heavy wood from the stack at the back door. I rolled up some newspaper tightly and laid it beneath the wood, remembering to leave room for the fire to breathe.

In a few minutes the fire blazed up eagerly and its warmth rushed out to me. I settled down on the sofa, turned out the lights, pulled my sweater around me, and gazed into the fire. These words came quickly, easily:

Tonight I watched the fire
Instead of TV
And it entertained me all evening.
No need to adjust the color
Or sound.
As I watched alone from the sofa
The fire sang to me
Talked to me
And cavorted.
Became serious and quiet,
Then burst forth in wild acrobatics.
I watched enthralled
Delighted
Amused
Satisfied.
The fire danced its heart out for
Me.
Just for me!
When sleep threatened
I fought to watch the fire just a little longer.
And even when my eyes finally shut,
Still it whispered to me in soft syllables
Of gratitude.

Father, it's amazing what You show me out my kitchen window. Thank You that we got to know the Farmers. I'll never forget them, their deep contentment and their kindness to us. I never imagined I'd grieve over them like this, but they taught me so much about life and love and what really matters.

PART SIX

"AND THERE BE NO CATTLE IN THE STALLS..."

23 | RELEASED

JEREMY WAS MAKING PROGRESS in his rehabilitation, and I knew that it wouldn't be much longer before he was released from Mulberry Grove. He still limped, but the orthopedist thought that would clear up with time. His new psychiatrist had prescribed medications that seemed to be controlling his illness. I wondered if he would take them on his own. It was one thing to have someone bring you pills and a glass of water, and another thing to be responsible for taking them yourself. And bipolar patients often think they don't need to continue their medication.

Jeremy seemed to like the counselor he saw at the psychiatrist's office. "I cried in there today," he told me one day when I picked him up.

I reached over to the passenger seat and hugged him. "Jeremy, that's wonderful. That means you're getting down to some real issues."

"That's what she said." He smiled faintly. We drove in silence, and then, looking straight ahead, he asked, "Do you ever think I'll be normal?"

Our eyes met. "I hope not. Not totally. Normal people are so dull, and besides, I don't have any normal friends. But I do believe you'll fit in. You'll be happy and enjoy life."

"I don't feel like it right now. I still feel scared sometimes, and life is too hard. I've lost so much—everything . . ."

I didn't want to lecture him about the bad decisions he'd made, so I tried to be positive. "Look at what you've gained. You finally know what's wrong. It's treatable. You walked away from five wrecks—"

"Six."

"Six wrecks. There are people who sincerely want to help you. Your company has been long-suffering. You still have good insurance. You can start over somewhere in a neat, clean, new place."

"I don't have much to start with. My whole landscaping business is gone . . ."

"You were in over your head. You took on more than anyone could do. Go slow."

"That's what my counselor says: 'Take baby steps.'"

"Sounds good to me."

I was grateful for our brief but honest conversation. Jeremy could disappear behind a wall and there was no way to get over it or under it. But now he was silent, and I had learned not to push him to talk more than he wanted to.

Jeremy's days at Mulberry Grove were coming to an end, but there were still some surprises left before they did. One day I walked into Jeremy's room. There was a Braves game on that day, so I was surprised to find him alone, staring at the ceiling. "Why aren't you watching the game with Bobby? Is he sick?" I asked. I looked out Jeremy's open door over to Bobby's room. His door was closed.

"He's gone," Jeremy said.

"What? You're teasing."

"No. They made him get his stuff and leave. His son just came to get him. Some of his stuff is still in his room. Go look for yourself."

I walked over to Bobby's room and knocked. There was no

answer. I opened the door. The room was mostly empty. His clothes were gone, but the TV was still there. His slippers still stuck out from under his bed.

I walked back to Jeremy's room.

"Told you, didn't I?"

"I'm sorry, Jeremy. Really sorry."

"Me too. He was my friend."

"He's still your friend."

"Yeah. He left me his home number."

"What happened?"

"You know Bobby. He'd been warned time and time again not to make a scene and upset the others. He scared some people."

"You'll soon be gone too. Will you miss Mulberry Grove?"

He thought for a moment and looked at me, "Yeah, I think I will. It's not so bad here. And the food's good."

On my way out, several of the ladies sitting in the lobby called me over. One of them smiled from behind her glasses, "That son of yours is so fine! We all love him and hate to see him leave. He's such a gentleman."

I savored every word. These older people brought out the very best in Jeremy. He'd smile and speak to each of them and always say, "Yes, ma'am" or "No, ma'am." He knew them all by name.

Jeremy's house had been sold, and he was apprehensive about where he'd live once he got out of Mulberry Grove. On her daily walks, Julie had found a new apartment complex near her house. She thought it might be just the place for Jeremy. The ground-floor apartment she'd looked at was perfect. The walls were off-white with beige trim, and there was beige carpeting. The apartment had a bedroom, a tiny office, and a kitchen with brand-new appliances and a large pantry. Gene, Julie, Jeremy, and I rode out to see it. It even smelled new.

Jeremy wasn't used to making decisions. For nearly a year other people—doctors, lawyers, family—had been making them for him. He put down a deposit and then stewed about it.

Finally, during the last part of September, he moved in. His leg and hip hurt if he stood on them too much. While Julie took him to a doctor's appointment, I put the finishing touches on the apartment. I stocked the kitchen with food, bought a comforter and bed linens and made the bed, put his books in the shelves, and put away most of his clothes. Then I turned down the bed and switched on a sleep machine I'd brought that played the sound of crickets and outside night noises. It was after dark when I drove back home to Watkinsville, about an hour away, so I wasn't there when Julie brought him home. The next day, she phoned to tell me about it. "It felt like home," Julie said. "After all that had happened to him in the old place, all the bad feelings, this new place felt just fantastic."

Earlier Gene and I had taken Jeremy to buy a car—the doctor said he was in good enough shape to drive. Jeremy loved to car shop. He talked the people at the dealership down quite a bit and drove away in a dark green Toyota 4Runner—not as fancy as some cars he'd driven, but paid for. His license was renewed and the car was insured.

He was still on probation for digging up a tree at four o'clock one morning when he was manic. Of all the things he'd ever done, to be arrested for that seemed surreal. After his court appearance, Jeremy had laughed and said, "The police told me, 'Jeremy, if you'd left the tree there and run, you could have gotten away, but no, you had to pick up the tree and try to take it with you. That's why we caught you.'" Someone pressed charges, and Jeremy was fined and put on probation. Whatever else he didn't remember to do, he never forgot to check in with the probation officer and pay off his fine.

When Julie phoned to tell me how good it felt in his place I soaked up her words, imagining Jeremy in his new apartment, and hoping and believing things would work out for him. I tried not to remember the night he spent with us after getting out of the behavioral facility when all of this had begun. . . .

Jeremy's medications weren't monitored at our house, and most of the time he seemed afraid, and he was always hungry. Gene was afraid that we couldn't manage Jeremy. I told him to go on to bed and I'd stay up with my son.

Jeremy looked terrified when he crawled into bed. I sat with him until he drifted off to sleep, and then went to bed. I hadn't been asleep long when I was awakened by noises in Jeremy's room. I hurried in; he was confused and frightened and insisted on getting into the tub. Then he climbed out soaking wet, wrapped a sheet around himself, and tumbled back onto the bed. I got him up and turned the mattress, hoping Gene wouldn't wake up. He wouldn't understand Jeremy's behavior. I didn't either, of course. But I just kept thinking, *It will get better.*

A little while later I got out of bed again. Jeremy had gone to the kitchen to get some brownies. Chocolate crumbs were all over the kitchen, and a trail led back to his bedroom. The sheets were wet again; he'd taken another bath. He said he felt safe in the bathtub. *Things always seem worse at night,* I told myself. *Tomorrow will be better. It has to be.*

In the morning Gene said, "We have to find some place that can care for him. Call somewhere."

"There's not any place, Gene! He has to try to get better. Give the meds a chance."

Gene was adamant. I made phone call after phone call, but there really wasn't any place that would take him.

Mercifully, Jeremy slept for the next two days and nights. I phoned the doctor, and in time his medications were streamlined, but after he started feeling better, he thought he didn't need them. When I gave them to him, that was fine, but taking them on his own was an entirely different matter.

Jeremy tried to go back to work. I got up at five in the morning with him, fixed him a bite to eat, and talked with him in the kitchen. I could see his fear. It was freezing cold, so he bundled up and then limped out to his car to drive an hour and a half to work.

While he was gone, I prayed a lot. I prayed that he'd be able to do the work and that he'd come back safely. One day when he didn't return until after dark, with no explanation of where he'd been, I questioned him closely.

"I'm not a child, Mom. Leave me alone," he snapped. His eyes didn't look right. After he went to work the next day, I found a small silver-gray can under his bed—an aerosol cleaner he used to get high. We found more cans out in the bushes where he parked his car. When he came home that night and Gene and I confronted him, he lied to us. Looking us right in the eyes, he said, "I haven't been huffing. Y'all are imagining it. I don't do that anymore." I pulled out the pile of cans, and we all stared at them silently.

Now, living on his own in his new apartment, Jeremy had been slowly making progress, bit by bit. He'd started to like his counselor and enjoyed attending the small group sessions she led at her office. He went to church, either with Julie and her family or with us. Julie saw him every day once he moved in to his new place. She fed him, hung out with him, talked to him, encouraged him, and washed his clothes. At his counselor's request, she even went to counseling with him. Jeremy trusted her more than any of us, and she knew him inside and out. It was almost as if they were children again, and she was caring for her little brother for me.

One day she phoned and said, "Guess what?"

"I don't know," I said. "But I hope it's something good. Even half-way good."

"Jeremy's not crazy anymore."

"What?"

"He's not, Mom. He's making jokes again. He was laughing like when he was small. He's going to be okay. I know it."

In my entire life, those were perhaps the sweetest words I'd ever heard.

Thank You, Lord, that Jeremy's better, that he's adjusting. Help me believe in him and trust You to help him. Help me not to hover.

MAMA'S PLAN | 24

My FIRST THOUGHT for an instant was: *I can't wait to tell Mother this good news.* Of course, the thought only lived briefly; my mother had been dead for nearly two years. Sometimes, though, I so wanted to share good things with her. She could get as excited as a teenager right up until she died at ninety-two. She was a strong woman who beat cancer three times. I'd never known her to be afraid of anything.

After my father died suddenly of strep throat in 1938, when I was not quite two, Mother went to work in a small bank on the town square in Elberton. She worked there for thirty-eight years. No matter what the weather, she'd walk to work, come home for a bite to eat, go back to work, and come home at night and make it look like fun. One of my fondest memories is of watching for her to come home late in the afternoon. On summer days I'd sit out on the curb and look way up Myrtle Street. I could see her turn from Church Street and start down the hill home. I'd run up the street to meet her and then we'd walk home to 153 Myrtle Street together, usually holding hands. I'd talk a mile a minute, and she'd hang on to every word. She was the best listener in the whole world.

Through the years, my mother taught me by her actions. I suppose I thought nothing about it at the time. Only when I became a mother myself did I realize what a remarkable single parent she had been. I suppose I was an average child, but she always made me feel special. I don't recall ever seeing her first thing in the morning or at the bank where I stopped by each day after school for a hug that her face didn't light up like a sunrise when she looked at me. How I wish I'd been able to mother as she had.

I suppose it was the reality of my first grandchild, Jamie, starting school that triggered the bittersweet memories of my own first year of school. "Miss Edna" was that marvelous old-fashioned kind of teacher who gladly put her entire life into teaching. I loved school: the smell of chalk and colored crayons, the way the old wooden floors smelled after Jim the janitor had waxed them, and having my own desk that was just my size. There was, however, one overwhelming problem with school—Mildred.

Every day when I walked the short distance home after school, Mildred would taunt and hit me. I was absolutely terrified of her. She had failed first grade and was a year older than I. Mildred didn't have any friends, so she seemed to concentrate on making enemies. Because I was one of the smallest children in first grade, she had selected me as her enemy number one.

As we walked home after school, she would step on my heels, making my shoes slide down. Then, when I stopped to adjust them, Mildred would slap me hard on the back. As soon as the dismissal bell rang each day, my heart started to pound and I blinked fast so I wouldn't cry.

Pretty soon my mother figured out that something was wrong at school. I didn't want to tell her about Mildred. I sat close to the radio listening to *The Lone Ranger*, pretending not to hear her questions about school. Mother continued to question me, and finally I sobbed out the whole story. "You can't do anything, Mama. You *can't*. Everyone will think I'm a baby."

It was impossible for Mother to pick me up after school. She had to work. I couldn't imagine what my mother might do. I was certain there was no answer—no answer at all for a problem this big.

The next day at school, Miss Edna leaned over my desk and whispered, "Marion, dear, could you stay after school and help me with a project? I spoke with your mother last evening, and she said it would be fine with her." Her blue eyes were understanding, and she smelled like Jergens hand lotion. I decided right then and there that all angels must have blue eyes and smell like Jergens hand lotion. I nodded eagerly.

I remained joyfully at my desk when the dismissal bell rang. Mildred looked confused for a bit, but filed out with the others. After a while Miss Edna said that I'd better be going on home. She stood on the front steps of the school and waved to me. I skipped up the hill without any fear whatsoever. Then, just as I got to the top of the hill, I heard familiar footsteps behind me. Mildred had waited for me. She immediately stepped on the back of my shoe and slapped my back. I cried; I couldn't help it.

When my mother saw my face after she got home from work, she questioned me. I begged not to go to school, and I didn't sleep much that night. The next morning she said brightly, "Marion, I'm going to walk up the hill with you today. I believe we'll see Mildred." Mildred walked from way across town to school. She never bothered me on the way to school, only afterward.

"Oh, Mama, please don't do that! Don't say anything to Mildred. It will just make her mad. Let me stay home by myself. Please, Mama."

"Hurry and get dressed, Marion." Her voice was gentle but firm. She smiled as though the problem were already solved.

"Ple-e-ease, Mama."

"Trust me, Mannie. I have a plan." My insides were in turmoil.

Why couldn't my mother understand that no plan she had dreamed up was going to work? We headed up Myrtle Street. Maybe we wouldn't see Mildred, I hoped. But my mother had this confident look. I knew the look well, and I had a sinking feeling that we would see Mildred and that Mother would use her plan.

Sure enough, just as we got to the top of the hill, we spotted Mildred. We waited a few horrible moments as she approached. She pretended not to see us.

"Hello, Mildred," Mother said quietly. Mildred stopped, frozen as still as a statue. Her hands and face were bright red from the intense cold. Her oversized coat hung open. There were only two buttons on it; the rest were missing. Underneath she wore a cotton dress, as though it were summer. I was so bundled up I could hardly walk.

Mother stooped down to Mildred's level. She didn't say anything at first. Instead, she rapidly buttoned Mildred's coat and turned the collar up around her neck. Then she fastened back the stubborn piece of hair that forever hung in Mildred's face. I stood off to one side watching our breath lingering in front of our faces in the frigid morning air, praying that no students would happen by and that my mother's plan would be over quickly.

"I'm Marion's mother. I need your help, Mildred." Mildred looked intently at my mother with an expression I couldn't identify. Their faces were inches apart. My mother's gloved hands held Mildred's cold ones as she spoke. "Marion doesn't have any brothers or sisters. She sort of needs a special best friend at school. Someone to walk up the hill with her after school. You look like you'd be a fine friend for her. Would you be Marion's friend, Mildred?" Mildred chewed on her bottom lip, blinking all the time, and then nodded.

"Oh, thank you!" Mama said with confidence and gratitude. "I just know you are someone I can depend on." Then she hugged Mildred long and hard. She gave me a quick hug and called to us as though nothing unusual had happened. "Bye, girls. Have a good day." Mildred and I walked on to school, stiffly, like mechanical dolls, both staring straight ahead without speaking. Once I glanced over her way: Mildred was smiling! I'd never seen her smile before.

We walked up the hill each day after school together, and pretty soon we were talking, laughing, sharing secrets. Mildred started tying her hair back the way Mama had fixed it. Sometimes she even wore a hair ribbon. Someone sewed buttons on her coat, and she buttoned all of them and always wore the collar turned up. Somehow I started calling her, "Mil." Then the others did too, even Miss Edna.

"Hey, Mil, sit by me," someone called out at lunch. "No, Mil, sit with us," someone else begged. Mildred shot them a happy smile, but she always sat with me at lunch. My mother usually included something in my lunch especially for Mildred, even notes of gratitude. Mil always let me in front of her in the line at the water fountain.

Valentine's Day was a very important event in first grade back in the 1940s. We made huge valentine boxes and set them on our wooden desks for a valentine exchange. I pulled out an enormous valentine toward the end of the party. Everyone stood up to see better. It was store-bought and had obviously cost a lot. Most everyone had made their valentines from red construction paper, lace, and glue. *Ahhhs* and *ohhhs* floated out over the classroom and seemed to linger suspended in the air, as I opened the magnificent valentine. Printed neatly in bold red letters inside the card was: "From your best friend."

I looked over at Mil. She was sitting with her hands folded on top of her desk and smiling the biggest smile ever. She had a red ribbon in her hair. Mildred smiled a lot now. She was getting good grades now, too, and didn't stuff her papers inside her desk anymore. Her eyes darted over and met mine. Right then I knew my mother's plan had worked.

Lord, I didn't understand Mama's plan back in 1942, or for years afterward. But along the way You showed me where it came from— 1 Corinthians 13:4–8: "Love is patient . . . kind . . . does not act unbecomingly . . . is not provoked, does not take into account a wrong suffered . . . believes all things, hopes all things, endures all things. Love never fails." Thank You for Mama's plan—Your plan—that works in all kinds of impossible situations.

MAMA AND THE SILVER COMET | 25

DEFEAT HAD A HARD TIME ever catching up with Mama. When our ceiling sprang a huge hole during a terrible storm and I thought it was the end of the world as water poured into our small house, once again Mama had a plan. She crawled up on top of a chest of drawers with a big tub and started catching the water. She was laughing! "Get me more pans, Mannie, then call Mr. Lennie." Mr. Lennie was our landlord, and he was good about fixing things. I grabbed the pans and then spoke to the operator, Miss Lillian. "Quick, Miss Lillian, get Mr. Lennie! Our house is flooding!"

"Don't be scared, Mannie. We'll save all this nice rainwater and wash our hair with it. I used to do that all the time when I was a little girl." I brightened up somewhat and most of the trauma of the incident disappeared.

One of my all-time favorite memories happened when I'd started my first job in Atlanta after college. I often went home on the weekends to Elberton, about a hundred miles east. A few weeks earlier, a hometown boy I'd been dating, Jerry West, who was attending Virginia Polytechnic Institute, had asked my mother, eyeball to eyeball, "Would you let Marion come up to V.P.I. for our big dance weekend? Fats Domino is going to be there. I'd get her a nice room with a little lady who rents rooms. She could come up on the Silver Comet."

I couldn't imagine my mother allowing me to do such a thing. It was 1957, and most young girls I knew didn't go off unchaperoned for a weekend. But I knew she liked Jerry.

He waited, still looking right into Mama's eyes. I glanced back and forth apprehensively. Both of them smiled ever so slightly. "I don't see why not," Mama said. My mouth opened wide and Jerry lit up as if a light had gone on inside him. We went to the train station in Elberton right then and got my ticket.

Mama wanted me to have a new formal dress. I'd worked as a secretary for a few months since I'd been out of college, but I didn't have any extra money. She said I could select a dress in Atlanta and charge it to her. She assured me that she'd have it paid for quickly. She managed her modest salary well. "Get something really pretty, Mannie," she added excitedly.

I'd planned to look all over Atlanta until I found the perfect dress. Unbelievably, I discovered it almost immediately on my lunch hour. I went to one of the finest stores in the city, a small, exclusive store I'd never been in before. But Mama had a charge account there, she'd said. Inside the store on a mannequin was *my* dress. I stood mesmerized, not even hearing what the saleslady said to me. She repeated it louder: "May I help you?"

Without taking my eyes off the dress, I said in a hushed tone, "I want that dress." It was in my colors: champagne, beige, rust, and a darker beige, with a taffeta strapless top. And the skirt—oh, the skirt was a dream come true: layers and layers of short net ruffles so that it stood out majestically. It was the popular new ballerina length.

"Perhaps you'd like to look at other dresses. We have quite a nice selection in the back. Many are . . . reasonably priced," she suggested.

"No, *that's* my dress. I'll try it on."

She wasn't smiling when she announced, "It's over sixty dollars!"

Over sixty dollars! That was an enormous price back in 1957, so much more than Mama and I had talked about. I reached out and lightly touched a stiff net ruffle. "May I use your phone?"

"Local call?" She looked even grimmer.

"No. I'll reverse the charges."

I reached her at work in Elberton. She always answered the phone at the bank. "Hello, Mama! I found the dress. But Mama—it's *over sixty dollars!*"

A pause. By standing on tiptoe I could still see the dress from the telephone.

"Marion, I want you to get the dress. You'll always remember this weekend. It's going to be special."

"Mama, the saleslady thinks I should look at cheaper dresses," I said, lowering my voice.

"Let me speak with her, please, Mannie."

I held the phone out to the small, unsmiling woman with her arms folded stiffly about her waist. "My mama wants to talk to you." She pulled off an enormous earring and put the phone to her ear.

"Yes. Yes! Of course. Certainly, ma'am." The women's entire countenance and voice changed. She was smiling. She hung the phone up gently and said in a newfound, soft voice, "Come right this way, Miss Bond; I'll help you into the dress. Your mother wants you to have long gloves too. She's absolutely right, of course. The dress will be perfect with your auburn hair, dear."

Even barefoot, I knew at last how Cinderella felt. It was all I could manage not to waltz over the plush carpet. Several customers stopped and smiled. The saleslady stood with her hands clasped together, almost as though she were praying. Then she brought long ivory gloves that came up to my elbows. Mama had arranged for me to charge it all.

The next weekend I took the new dress home to Elberton for Mama to see. She loved it as much as I did. Then I returned to Atlanta to my job. Only one more week and my new dress and I would be on the Silver Comet headed to Virginia.

I was back in my apartment in Atlanta when Mama phoned. When I heard her say, "Oh, Mannie," I knew instantly. I could see the dress hanging on the back of her bedroom door in its clear zipped bag with the store name printed on it. How could I have forgotten it? I was to board the Silver Comet in Atlanta on Friday and ride overnight to Virginia.

My heart tumbled to my feet. I had to work all week. So did Mama. How would I get my Cinderella dress for the ball?

"I'll stop the train, Marion." Mama said firmly. She sounded confident, but how? The Silver Comet usually whizzed by my little hometown, blowing its horn frantically at the crossing. "Don't worry," Mama urged me once again.

But I did worry, all week. Suppose we just sped through Elberton? That's what the train did when no one got on or off. How could I go to the big dance without my once-in-a-lifetime dress?

Then it was Friday. I was on the train speeding toward Elberton. Worrisome thoughts seemed to speed through my mind, over and over. After a while, in the late afternoon sun I began to see sweetly familiar landmarks. My heart thumped loudly. On the outskirts of town I recognized houses and the giant oak trees. Then there were the granite sheds, tin buildings that appeared to be hurriedly thrown together. They didn't look like much, but beautiful cemetery markers were carved in those sheds. Granite lay buried underneath many parts of Elberton. We were known as "the granite center of the South." My heart suddenly felt like granite, heavy and cold. We were getting close to the train station. *Can Mama really do it?*

I sat on the very edge of my seat, biting my lip, trying to decide if the train was slowing down. Was it? Or was it simply my deep longing? The scenes outside didn't seem to be passing by as rapidly. It was slowing down! The train screeched to a glorious halt!

I looked outside. There it was—the Elberton Depot. It had never looked so wonderful. The building was brick, with a slanted green roof and long windows; it looked like the miniature depots that came with toy train sets.

Suddenly everyone turned to stare. I did too. There was Mama! She shot me a victorious I-told-you-so smile, as though she stopped trains all the time. Mama came down the aisle like the Queen of England, holding my dress up high. The porter helped her find a place to hang it. She gave me a quick, hard hug and hurried off the train. Not a word had been spoken. It was all a beautiful, unforgettable pantomime.

The train rumbled to life again. I pressed my face to the window and waved joyfully, gratefully, as we continued on to Virginia. Mama stood waving back to me with both hands, smiling as always.

I still have that dress. My daughters and granddaughters have worn it to parties. I often go to the closet in the spare bedroom and just look at it or touch it. The magic remains.

I guess Mother was in her late eighties when I asked her, "Mama, how did you stop the Silver Comet that night?"

Her eyes sparkled. "The depot agent was a lifelong friend of mine. So I told him about your dress and asked if he would please stop the train. In small towns, people extend their friends . . . certain courtesies. Besides, you remember the verse, 'Ask and it shall be given you; seek, and you shall find'? It's true. So many times, all you have to do is ask."

Oh, Father, Mama was right again: All I have to do is ask. And I do, Father—for healing, for peace, for new life for my boys and me.

MAMA'S MOVE | 26

I POURED PRUNE JUICE into one small glass, cranberry juice into another. From five different boxes of cereal lined up on my kitchen counter, I measured precise amounts into a bowl and added sliced bananas, sugar, and milk. Then I arranged everything on a tray along with a napkin, silverware, and a fresh cup of coffee.

For four years, ever since Mother had come to live with Gene and me in Watkinsville after a recurrence of cancer at age eighty-five, I'd prepared the same breakfast. I could put it together with my eyes closed. . . .

Mother had been through two mastectomies, a year apart, when she was in her early seventies. The first cancer was discovered only a year after Jerry died. She came to my home in Lilburn, and I took her to Emory University Hospital where she had the first mastectomy, and then the second a year later. She smiled through the ordeal and went to the operating room calling out, "Mannie, have my makeup ready when I get back!" Mother's makeup was important to her, and she applied it like an expert. When she came to live with us and could no longer make it to the mall, the Estée Lauder representative came to our home.

She'd been cancer-free for nearly ten years when cancer showed up in her spine. We began seeing doctors. Cancer has a way of hurting a victim in all kinds of places, so we saw the eye doctor, the dentist, a radiologist and our family doctor, and had tests run almost every week.

My mother enjoyed the visits to the doctors. They were social outings for her, and she chatted about travel, clothes, or a holiday. Her health was always last on her list.

"On a scale of one to ten, how's your pain?" the doctor would ask.

"It varies." She'd smile. "I like your suit. Sharp looking. Four buttons on the cuff."

If she was afraid, I never saw it. While I was running one day, I prayed, "God, give me a word to encourage me." As I jogged, a word suddenly slipped into my thoughts. I immediately hated it. *Gone.*

"No, Lord, Not that word. I hate that word. Not gone—like Jerry was gone. Give me a word of encouragement—of hope. Don't give me a scary word."

It seemed to take forever, but just as I came huffing and puffing up my driveway, I thought I understood. *Listen, Marion. Gone—as in "The cancer is gone."*

I stood stock still, smiling. Had I heard correctly? Could I believe this?

I desperately didn't want to lose anyone else I loved to cancer. I thought there had to be a gentler death. I wasn't sure I could be the caregiver to someone else I loved with cancer.

Five years later, Gene and I sat in the waiting room while Mother had a spinal scan. I knew it was taking too long—not a good sign. Her oncologist suspected that the cancer might be spreading. Mother had flatly, but very politely, refused chemotherapy.

"No, dear, I'm not taking it," she said, smiling at the handsome young doctor.

"But you *have* to, Mrs. Grogan. It's the next step."

"No, no, no, not for me. Not at my age. Sorry." Her voice was adamant but bubbly. The doctor was less than happy with her decision, but he quickly regained his composure. She patted his hand and he gave her the familiar hug that had become a part of their visits.

Finally, the radiologist came from behind swinging doors and motioned me into the hall. My heart fell to my toes. They had done that with Jerry too. "Could I speak with you, please?" he asked with a smile. When everyone in a hospital starts becoming really sweet, it's not a good sign.

"Want me to go with you?" Gene said, starting to rise.

I shook my head and walked like a robot out into the hall. The doctor looked to the left and then the right and leaned over to whisper. "Can you verify that your mother hasn't had chemotherapy?"

"Certainly. She refused it!"

"Are you sure?"

"Absolutely."

"I could lose my job for telling you this, but we don't see the cancer. It's . . . it's . . . gone. We've never seen anything quite like it."

I started to squeal and jump up and down. But he cautioned, "Shhhhh."

"Thank you. Thank you. Thank you. Thank you." *Gone. Gone. Gone. Gone.* What a beautiful, fantastic, totally lovely word. *Gone.*

Carrying the tray, I walked carefully to Mother's bedroom. I paused at the closed door and glanced at the meal I was about to bring her. I remembered the breakfasts Mother had prepared for me long ago. I never had much appetite early in the day, so she tried to make breakfast special, adding raisins and brown sugar to my oatmeal, serving it in a special bowl decorated with a cheerful rooster.

The best part was that she sat at the breakfast table with me and told me a story while I ate. Even as a little girl, I understood those moments were daily blessings. Mother's job was our livelihood, and she put in long days at her office. She worked just as hard to make sure our relationship remained close—harder, truthfully—and she succeeded so well that to me, it seemed as if we'd been given all the time in the world together.

Now, these many years later, my mother and I were once again living under one roof. Things had gone well when she first moved in. I wasn't sure how or when it began, or even why, but gradually the distance and the tension grew between us. We talked less and Mother withdrew to her room more often. If it weren't for Veronica Hunter, the health-care worker who came by every day to look in on her and help her bathe and dress, Mother would've had almost no interaction with people. That worried me. I felt I was doing a poor job as a companion—and as a daughter.

I held the tray and glared at her bedroom door. Lately I'd been so frustrated I wanted to shout, "I can't stand this anymore, Mother! I want us to be close again." But I couldn't. We didn't have that kind of relationship. We'd hardly ever had a minor tiff, let alone a full-blown fight, and I wasn't about to start one now. Stifling a sigh, I knocked, then eased the door open. "Good morning, Mother."

"Good morning, dear!" she said. "Mannie," she murmured when she saw the tray, "you didn't have to go to all this trouble."

It was obvious she had gotten up early to put on makeup and brush her hair so she would be presentable when I came in. That was Mother, always putting on a good face—no matter what.

"Do you need anything else?" I asked.

"No, thank you. This is marvelous," she replied, giving me her patented smile. She spread the cloth napkin across her lap. That was my cue to leave, so I did, closing the door behind me.

Back in the kitchen I sank down at the table. Gene saw my expression and shook his head. I knew what was on his mind. For a while he'd been telling me, "You can't go on like this, Marion. You're not happy, and even though she never complains, I don't think your mother is either. This has been going on for four years now. You need to consider a change."

But how could I tell Mother our living together wasn't working anymore? She'd been unfailingly loving and gracious to me. Didn't I owe it to her to treat her the same way? Mother was as strong-willed and independent-minded as ever, but she could no longer live without a great deal of help from someone. Her walking was becoming almost impossible, and she'd fallen several times. Once she stayed on the floor for nearly six hours, and when we came in I demanded, "Why didn't you call? The telephone was right near you."

Lying on the floor, she smiled at Gene and me and said, "I'm fine. Just help me up so I can go to the bathroom."

There was no one else but me, and she didn't want anyone other than me looking after her. Other than me and Gene, that is. She adored him.

I loved my mother to the point of fierceness for all she'd done for me. She made sure I wanted for nothing growing up. She led a rather dull life, I suppose, but she shared the details with me, and it always sounded exciting. She devoted so much attention to me that I never felt as if I were missing out because I didn't have both parents around. Why then couldn't I give her what she needed now? I longed for her to have new stories, new friends, new experiences. She deserved to be living a richer life, not spending her days closeted in her room.

Veronica, making her usual house call, let herself in, and her voice rang out like the most comforting sound of the day. Here was sweet relief. My mother adored Veronica, and Veronica liked and understood my mother. She gave me her usual bright, sincere smile and headed toward Mother's room. I heard the two of them talking and laughing like old friends after nearly four years together. *Mother should be enjoying herself like this all the time,* I thought guiltily.

On her way out Veronica caught me brooding. "Marion, you might not want to hear this," she began, "but I have to say it; it just doesn't feel right in this house anymore. Your mother needs to be in her own place. I told her so today."

My mouth fell open. It hurt to hear that, but at the same time I felt a tremendous, unexpected sense of relief. Maybe now Mother and I could get the whole thing out in the open.

The next day when I brought her breakfast, I asked as nonchalantly as I could manage, "What do you think of Veronica's suggestion?"

"What suggestion?" Mother said, snapping her napkin open in her lap.

Taking a deep breath, I replied, not understanding really how I was managing to do it, "About your moving into your own place . . . a home where you can mix with other folks."

"Forget it!" she declared, in a voice the whole neighborhood could probably hear. "I'm not moving."

"But, Mother, you might like—-"

"Leave me alone."

"That's the problem," I said. "You're a people person. You're not made to spend all day alone. And I worry about what this is doing to us."

"You don't seem worried to me."

"Well, I am. We hardly talk, and we're getting short with each other."

"Then I'll go back to my house in Elberton," Mother said.

"You can't live on your own anymore," I reminded her. She glared at me. "Mother, please give this some thought," I said. "Okay?"

Although she didn't answer, when I closed her door behind me, the tension between us didn't seem as impenetrable as before. We'd actually had our version of a fight and it wasn't as bad as I had dreaded.

I made inquiries about a new assisted-living home just around the corner from us. I told Mother that they were having a picnic the following Saturday. I showed her the handsomely printed invitation I'd picked up at the home. She glanced at it, then flung it into her wastebasket. "I'm not about to go to some picnic for pathetic old ladies nobody wants."

"Gene and I want you to come with us," I said. I walked over to her closet. "What would you wear?"

"Oh, just shut up," she snapped.

She'd never said anything like that to me before, but this was the spunky mother I loved. "You know what?" I said, hiding a smile. "You're never going to turn into a pitiful old lady. That's just not you." I hung the outfit I'd given her the previous Mother's Day on the closet door, a silent ultimatum—we *would* attend that picnic.

Folding her arms, Mother regarded me coolly. "If you and Gene are set on going to that picnic," she allowed, "I guess I might as well go along."

When I went to her room Saturday morning, Mother was waiting, perfectly made-up, coiffured, and dressed in the outfit I'd given her, looking like a *Modern Maturity* cover girl.

At the picnic we were greeted by the tangy aroma of barbecue and the sound of "Georgia on My Mind." I saw a smile cross Mother's lips. Then she started waving eagerly. Two ladies at a picnic table by us waved back. "Jewette Grogan," they called to her. "You'd better be coming to sit by us!" They were old friends from Elberton. Gene and I went to get some food, and by the time we came back, so many people were enjoying Mother's company that I could hardly squeeze in at the table to hand her a plate.

Not long after that, Mother moved into a room that Gene and I decorated with some of her favorite things from her home in Elberton.

I was able to visit her daily, and honestly, I think we spent more time together after her move than when she was with us. I should have known our relationship was strong enough to survive even that test; after all, Mother had instilled in me the courage to do difficult things.

One afternoon, I was standing outside Mother's door, my hand lifted to knock, when an old familiar feeling came over me. Looking at the "BLESS THIS HOME" lace banner she'd hung on the door, I realized what it was: that same delicious sense of love and anticipation I felt blessed by years ago, every time I'd stop by the bank after school.

I knocked. "Come in," Mother called out.

When I walked into her room, her face lit up. "Mannie," she exclaimed, "I'm so glad to see you!"

I wasn't a bit surprised.

Father, You healed Mama's body just like You promised. And when our relationship was hurting, You healed that too. Help me hold on to Your promises, no matter what.

PART SEVEN

"Yet, I Will Exult in the Lord . . ."

27 | STRONG ENOUGH TO CRY

MOTHER LIVED FOR FOUR YEARS with Gene and me and two years in assisted living. She went to a nursing home when the doctor and I agreed that she wasn't able to function any longer in assisted living. Her oxygen level fell often, and she couldn't get up or do much of anything without help. But still the cancer remained gone.

She lived her last five days in a local hospital. One of the last things she said to me was, "Aren't you getting tired, Mannie?"

Mother died early on a Saturday morning in July. I still think her homegoing service was magnificent. The funeral home in Elberton was a restored antebellum house, with high ceilings, marble-top tables, and velvet-upholstered chairs. I loved the color scheme: pink and rose and a quiet green. I put pictures of Mother around the room and even displayed the straw hat with the pink ribbon that she wore when I wheeled her outside in her hot pink wheelchair.

And Mother looked beautiful. She wore the Mother's Day outfit I'd given her—the one she'd worn to the picnic two years earlier. It looked like a garden, with large but delicate roses. Gene found her long-time hairdresser in Elberton, and she came out of retirement to do Mother's hair. The florist knew how important color was to me and found roses that matched Mama's dress: pale pink, like sunset with gold woven in. We had several dozen in tall vases at the head and foot of the casket. She wore pearls, and in her hands—hands that could type faster than I'd thought possible; hands that always tied my sashes just so; hands that opened any gift I'd ever given her with excitement in every finger; hands that looked so much like my own—she held a linen handkerchief trimmed with lace. She had on her "earbobs"; she refused to call them anything else. She looked so young—the funeral director had done a fantastic job with makeup. Not heavy. The only thing missing—and I knew not to expect it—was her overwhelming smile.

Three weeks later Gene and I made another trip back to Elberton to take care of business. We had to go to the bank where she'd worked for thirty-eight years. As we drew near to Elberton, I felt an oppressive, almost physical sense of sadness creep over me, but I fought it off. I still hadn't cried, not through Mother's illness or her death or the funeral. I guess the tears were down in me somewhere, but they never surfaced. I didn't try to hold them back; they just stayed hidden.

We circled the neatly manicured town square, filled with marigolds and zinnias blooming lusciously in the summer heat. Gene reached over and took my hand, but I stared straight ahead like a store mannequin. He glanced at me. "Honey, is it too soon to do this?" he asked.

"Of course not," I said. "I can handle it." After all, my mother lived a long and happy life. She'd been in good health for most of her life and had devoted family and friends. She didn't die of cancer; her heart and her energy just wore out. My rational mind told me how fortunate she and I both had been, that death was a natural part of life. And so, being reasonable, I tried to push away the feelings that were almost smothering me. It certainly didn't make sense for me to break down now—I hadn't even cried at the cemetery. Mother would have wanted me to hold up.

"Ready to go to the bank?" Gene asked.

"Well, sure, that's what we came for."

We were headed for the fancy new building that housed the bank where Mother had been assistant vice president until she retired back in 1974. The original brick-and-granite bank still stood on the north corner of the square; now it was the headquarters of the town newspaper. That was the building I remembered from my childhood, the place where my mother worked.

When she first started working there, the bank had all of three employees—a president, a vice president and Mother, who did everything from sweeping the floor to shining the spittoons. Back then, I didn't think much about how Mother had to walk a mile and a half to work every day. I assumed that all mothers economized by digging into their lipsticks with a bobby pin to get the last bit of color.

She was tall, slim, beautiful. I loved being seen with her. She wore her thick dark hair pulled back, which accentuated her Clara Bow mouth and set off her dimples. She wore elegant second-hand tailored clothes, sent to her by my aunt in New York who did part-time modeling, and White Shoulders perfume, just a dab so a bottle would last forever. Until I was old enough to go to school, while Mother was at work I stayed with a next-door neighbor. When I felt the urge, I would lift the receiver off the tall black phone so I could tell the operator, "Number seven, please."

"Granite City Bank, Jewette Bond speaking," my mother would answer efficiently.

Those words thrilled me every time. "Hey, Mother," I'd say.

"Mannie!" she'd exclaim. "How's my girl?"

Now as Gene and I drove past the old bank building, I stared at the small ground-floor window that had looked into her office. After school, on the way to the drugstore for a cherry Coke, my friends and I would peek into the tiny window, shading our eyes from the sun's glare, and scratch on the screen. My mother would look up from the keys of her Royal typewriter, hop up from her swivel chair, open the heavy, glass front door and give me a hug. "How was your day, Mannie?"

Mother had Wednesday afternoon off, and that was my favorite time of the week. Most of all I remembered the sweltering summers, when there wasn't a breeze to stir our kitchen curtains. Mother and I thumped on the watermelons being sold from the back of a farmer's old truck until we found the perfect one. At home, Mother wore light blue shorts and went barefoot, just like me. She put a piece of newspaper on our kitchen table, heaved the melon on top, then cut into it. There was a satisfying splitting sound, and I stood on tiptoe to get the first glimpse of the rosy insides. We had picked a good one all right! We took the thick slices and sat on our back steps, sinking our faces into the juicy melon, laughing and spitting out seeds while the juice ran down our arms.

I could almost taste that long-ago sweetness as Gene and I drove through Elberton to the sleek new Granite City Bank—now called Regions Bank—blocks farther down from the main square. As long as I could remember, Mother had had a safe-deposit box in the bank, and it was one of the things she'd mentioned in the months before she died. "Remember the lockbox, Mannie," she said.

"I know, Mother," I'd say, rubbing lotion into her frail hands.

We parked, then Gene and I walked into the building. The air-conditioning gave out an almost arctic chill, but we were greeted warmly by the employees, many of whom had known my mother. I took a deep breath and forced myself to smile. *It would be so embarrassing to cry in front of them.*

One of the cashiers showed us into the area where lockboxes covered the walls. She handed me a big manila envelope. "You can put everything in this," she said. Gene helped me open the box. I emptied its contents into the huge envelope—a jumble of bank books, wrinkled papers, old coins, photographs, and a box rattling with jewelry. I felt my throat tightening. "Don't you want to look at what's there?" Gene asked.

"Later," I said.

When we got back in the car, I sagged with relief. Thank goodness I hadn't broken down or gotten emotional! As Gene started driving, I reached into the envelope and pulled out a letter on onionskin paper, yellowed with age. I unfolded the pages and looked at the date on the top: June 27, 1938, just after my father died.

"My Precious Baby," it began. I held my breath as I read down the page. "Mannie, you were a baby wanted very badly by both your daddy and mother." As far as my mother was concerned "a better soul never lived" than my daddy. She went on to tell how happy they had been together because they understood each other perfectly.

I read on, blinking rapidly, "Mother wishes you a very happy life. I hope and pray a lot of good things will come your way. May God watch over you and keep you always. To me, your being here is the dearest thing on earth. With all my love, Mother."

I held the yellowed pages in my hand, overcome by emotion. This was a letter that my mother had meant for me to read when she was gone.

"You hungry?" Gene asked. Without waiting for an answer, he pulled into the parking lot of a fast food restaurant. Parked alongside the entrance was an old beat-up truck, its bed piled high with watermelons, just like the trucks when I was a child. "Gene! Watermelons! Let's get a big one!"

Gene was concentrating on lunch. "Not now, honey," he said. "It might split and make a mess." He hopped out of the car and headed toward the restaurant. For a moment I sat there stunned. Maybe I'd just sit in the awful heat and slowly melt like a stick of butter. *Lord, what's the matter with me?*

"Marion?" It was Gene calling from the restaurant doorway, looking puzzled. *Breathe,* I told myself. *Move.* I stuffed the letter into the envelope, got out of the car as if in a trance, went in, and sat at a table. Gene was ready to get in line and order. "What do you want, honey?"

"Nothing," I murmured. Gene came back with his hamburger and fries. I just sat there, desperately trying to reason with my emotions. *Oh, Lord, what grown woman falls apart in the middle of McDonald's because she can't have a watermelon? Help me keep it together.* I tilted my head back to keep the tears in my eyes, fighting to regain composure. I lost the battle. As people around us kindly looked away, I crumpled. I buried my face in my hands and began to cry, hard, from a place deep inside, a place where my love for Mother was rooted. She must have experienced a similar wrenching grief when Daddy died. She had been strong. Yet my aunt Liz had told me how Mother had cried after Daddy's funeral.

It seemed an eternity until I uncovered my face. Gene held out his handkerchief. "It's okay, Marion," he said. "Can I get you anything?"

"Yes," I told him.

In an instant Gene was up and out the door. I watched from the window as he handed some money to the man at the watermelon truck, then opened our trunk so he could lift the watermelon in.

I ran to the door, "Put it up front with me!" I cried, then rushed to the car and climbed in. I slipped off my sandals and propped my bare feet on the watermelon's cool skin. I knew the pain and grief I'd felt pressing on my heart would never go away altogether. Why should they? The more you love, the more loss hurts. But as we drove past the old bank building for the last time, new feelings stirred inside me—peace, acceptance, understanding. Mother was gone, but God would help me endure. Still, I could cry when I needed a good, thorough cleansing. Love makes loss hard. But it also makes us strong—strong enough to cry.

Father, You taught me that refusing to acknowledge my pain is a sign of weakness, not strength. Don't let me forget that when I'm hurting, I can always cry on Your shoulder.

THAT DAY NO | 28
ONE WANTS
TO REMEMBER

ONLY MONTHS AFTER MOTHER'S DEATH, Jerry's parents, Ada and Robert West, who lived in Elberton, became ill and couldn't live alone any longer. They had stayed in their own home much longer than they should have. Things were going downhill fast as they often do with older folks determined to preserve their independence.

Jerry's only sibling, Allen, seven years older than Jerry, had died about ten years earlier. Allen had experienced a mental breakdown his freshman year in college in North Carolina. The diagnosis, when they finally got one, was as bad as it gets: paranoid schizophrenia. He'd spent most of his adult life in a mental hospital and then in a group home in Virginia, where the Wests had lived before coming to Elberton in 1953.

They made the difficult decision to leave Allen in Virginia because the facility he was in was considered excellent and the move would be traumatic for him. So Jerry's mom and dad made trips to Virginia every three months to take Allen out for a two-hour excursion.

When Allen died in his late sixties, Jerry had been dead for more than a decade. Both the Wests' children were gone, and there were no close relatives nearby. So when the Wests needed full-time care, we decided that they should go to Mulberry Grove, where my mother had been until her death. Within a year, Ada and Robert were also dead.

With all the Wests gone, I allowed myself to remember May 17, 1982, a day we had all determined to forget and rarely spoke about, but was still crystal clear in my memory.

We knew Jerry's dad was going through some mental battles. Jerry's mom, who never phoned us—she never wanted to bother anyone—called several times a day, day after day. They were urgent calls.

"Jerry, I don't know what to do. Your daddy—something's terribly wrong. He's dirty from working in the garden, and he's packing all his things in the car and saying he has to drive to Virginia to kill Allen. Jerry . . . he's . . . he's—" The line went dead.

I was standing by Jerry. We'd been dressing to go to a spring party—an outdoor garden party—and I was about to put on my new dress. We were in a festive mood.

"Mother, we'll be right there," Jerry said. Elberton was an hour away.

Jerry was grim. I'd never seen him grim; he was the eternal optimist. I'd never seen him worry or have a headache or complain, except about a football game when his team didn't win. He made the best of everything.

He explained without looking at me what his mother had said, and I dropped my new dress over a chair and slipped into jeans. He changed clothes, and we got into the car. Jeremy and Jon, thirteen then, went with us.

We often went to Elberton to see the Wests and my mother, but this trip was horribly different. We drove in silence. When we were three blocks from the house, Jerry pulled under the shade of a huge oak tree. My heart was thumping wildly. "We have to pray, Marion," he said. "We're going into something we don't know how to handle." He held my hands and prayed, "God, go before us and with us. Help us do what we have to do, what we can't possibly do on our own. Protect everyone. . . ."

We drove up to the house, where we saw a police car and some other vehicles. Robert's car was so full of stuff that there was hardly room for a driver. We pulled into the backyard and went into the house through the back door. The first thing we saw was that Robert had pulled the phone out of the wall.

We found him in the den. Gun in hand, he started to lunge for Jerry. Jerry grabbed him quickly, forcing Robert to drop the gun. They both fell to the floor.

In the adjoining living room, Ada stood wringing her hands. Her face was twisted in agony, but she shed no tears. Two policemen stood near her.

Jerry sat on his father's legs. "Sit on his chest," he said to me. "Hold him down."

Robert hadn't bathed or shaved for several days. His eyes weren't the eyes of the man we knew. "I'm going to kill Allen," he said. "I have to. I can't let him suffer any more. I'll kill you all as soon as I can get up. Get out of my house! This is *my* house! No one asked you here. Get out, I tell you!"

As the policemen moved toward us to help, Jerry motioned them back. "Let us try," he mouthed. For some reason, they did. I can't remember if they went outside then or later. I just remember sitting on top of my father-in-law, looking into his menacing eyes, and hearing him tell me that he was going to hurt me.

Jeremy hid behind a huge overstuffed chair and didn't make a sound. Jon stayed in a back bedroom. To this day, I don't know what he heard or did. He's never wanted to talk about it.

Jerry started to pray out loud, and I joined him. Jerry claimed the promise in Isaiah 55:17: "No weapon that is formed against you shall prosper." "I'm going to kill you, too, Ada," Robert bellowed.

The whole thing must have lasted for a half an hour or maybe longer. I had no sense of time. I only knew that we were in a battle for our lives and prayer was the only answer.

Jerry continued to pray, and I joined in loudly, louder than Robert screamed. We called on all the forces of heaven to intervene. We didn't know what we were doing; God seemed to be giving us directions one horrifying second at a time. We both chose to trust Him and somehow—and I'll never know how—we believed with all our hearts that God was going to show us what to do. We were not to surrender.

Suddenly the struggle was over. Robert looked spent, weary, and nearly normal. He yawned again and again. Jerry cautiously got up and motioned for me to get up also. We watched Robert crawl over to the sofa, pull himself up and sag onto it, drained and harmless.

"Allen, oh, Allen," he cried weakly. "My poor son."

"Daddy," Jerry said softly, sitting by me on the floor, about two feet away from his father. "You have another son. I love you."

"Allen, Allen." Robert wailed. Ada still waited in the den, watching us. I think the police were outside—at any rate, I couldn't see them. Someone had picked up the gun.

"I love you, Daddy," Jerry said, crying now.

Jerry's saying this was every bit as strange as our terrific struggle with Robert. These men didn't display affection or talk about their feelings. They never talked about Allen. For years we didn't even mention his name. Then one day, I asked Ada if I could send him a Christmas gift. After that, we sent Allen gifts on occasion, and Ada would talk with me about him, even show me pictures of him, hidden way down in the bottom of a cedar chest. We only talked about Allen when Jerry and Robert were away. After a while, Ada would smile as she talked about him. "Before he got sick," she always added.

Robert ignored Jerry; I could hardly believe it. "Daddy, Daddy? Do you hear me?" Jerry said. He crawled over to Robert and held onto him.

Robert kept yawning and saying Allen's name over and over. "Daddy," Jerry said loudly. "I'm telling you that I love you. Can you hear me? Do you love me? I need to hear you say it, Daddy. I've needed it for a long time. Please tell me, Daddy, please." Jerry was sobbing now. I'd never seen him cry.

Oh, Lord, please let Robert see Jerry and look him right in the eyes and tell him how much he loves him. Jerry has to have that. He has to.

Robert never looked at Jerry, not once. Mostly, he stared at the ceiling. Jerry's sobs grew quieter. He didn't beg any longer.

After a long silence, we started trying to put things back together, except for the phone, which would have to be reconnected. The police were gone. The gun was gone. The washing machine was going. Ada had started unpacking Robert's things from the car. She smiled a bit now, and somehow we were talking about food.

We sat out in the backyard under the old pecan tree in the aluminum chairs with seats that Robert had rewoven himself. "No need to buy new ones," he'd laughed. He didn't like to spend money unnecessarily.

We sat there talking and drinking the lemonade that Ada had made. Jon and Jeremy stood close to their daddy and said nearly nothing. Jerry and his daddy joked and did imitations of people we all knew. Somehow, we laughed, even me. I began to wonder if I might be losing my mind. The whole day had been so unreal.

Then we were back in our green station wagon driving back to Lilburn as if the visit had been normal. I looked at Jerry; he seemed so different—no big smile or happy, booming voice.

Something terrible happened today. I don't know what just yet. But this isn't over. Our lives are going to change. Jerry is changing right before my eyes. I'm going to hate this date, May 17, 1982. I hate it already.

That night Jerry tossed in bed and whimpered like a small child. He cried out several times. He had always been a sound sleeper; nothing had ever bothered him before. The next two nights were the same. When he finally decided to talk about it, he said, "Marion, I don't know what to do. My daddy could kill my mother or himself. I know I should have him declared incompetent. We should go to a lawyer in Elberton and . . ."

So we drove to Elberton and parked in front of Robert's lawyer's office. We got out of the car and started to walk to the office, but after a few steps, I found I was walking alone. Jerry stood perfectly still halfway up the walk. "I can't do this," he said. So we got back in the car and drove the hour back to Lilburn.

The next day I went to the dentist. As I was going into the dentist's office, Julie's husband, Ricky, came driving up, got out of the car, and hurried up to me. "Hi, Ricky," I said. "What are you doing here?"

"Robert's shot himself."

"Robert who?" I asked. We knew lots of Roberts in Lilburn. I didn't for one second think it was Robert West.

But it was Robert West. He'd shot himself in the head out in his shop behind the house. The ambulance had come, and he was in the hospital. He'd put the gun to his head and fired.

At the hospital an astonished doctor told us, "I don't understand it at all. The bullet entered his head, but went . . . flat. He's okay physically. We'll keep him on the psychiatric floor for a while."

The next moment we were visiting with Robert, who smiled as though he'd been admitted for an ingrown toenail and said, "I'm fine. I'm coming home."

Five days later, he did. Somehow he got people to do whatever he wanted.

Jerry still seemed to be torn by his responsibility for his father. We knew Robert took lithium and some other medications, although no one ever talked about it. Jerry went to his parents' house and wrote down all Robert's prescriptions. When he got back home, he phoned one of the best psychiatrists in Atlanta and made an appointment.

When we saw the doctor, Jerry briefly explained what had happened and then showed him the medication list. "Do these sound right to you?" he asked.

The doctor studied the list and nodded his head. "This is exactly what I would prescribe. Was he drinking, by any chance, when he . . . had the episode?"

"He doesn't usually drink," Jerry answered.

I chimed in. "He was drinking that day. He smelled of it. I found a bottle in his car."

"Alcohol should never be taken with these medications," the doctor said quickly.

We resumed our lives as they'd been before, although nothing seemed "as before" to me. I wanted to talk, to ask Robert and

Ada questions, to talk to his doctors. But instead, we had our usual superficial conversations when we visited them: nothing serious—ever.

Then, on September 9, Jerry had his first grand mal seizure. We were in our car, on the way to see Jon play football; Jeremy was in the backseat. For more than six weeks, the doctors tried to discover the cause of his initial seizure and the others that followed. Late in October they decided to do exploratory brain surgery. I tried as hard as I knew how to believe everything would be okay.

When the surgery was over, the surgeon asked to see our whole family in a conference room. All I wanted was for my husband to be okay, for life to be normal again. I wouldn't argue about anything: I'd learn to love football, and I'd watch Jerry reading the sports page happily. I'd never complain again. I'd even help him in the garden, and I'd put the vegetables he grew in the freezer—something he'd wanted but I'd refused to do. If he'd just live.

We sat around a huge shiny table—Julie and Jen and Jon and Jeremy; Julie's husband, Ricky; Ada and Robert; my mother. We sat and waited for the doctor. He walked in quickly, not looking at any of us. He had changed out of his surgical scrubs into a nice sports coat and slacks and expensive-looking shoes. He was detached, professional.

"Glioblastoma multiforme, grade four," he said. "It's red hot. He has a few months at the most."

I fixed my eyes on a clock on the wall as I felt myself turn to stone. I felt hard and cold. I watched the second hand as I had in the delivery room when our girls had been born and then the twins. It was the same kind of clock.

I have no idea why I refused to show emotion. I blinked my eyes and kept looking at the clock and felt like I'd turned into a rock. I didn't want to feel anything.

"Do you have any questions?"

The others asked questions. I don't remember what.

"Mrs. West. Do you have any questions?" the doctor asked. I don't think he looked at me. I didn't look at him.

"When do you think it started?" I heard myself ask.

I wasn't sure he'd give me an answer, but he did, quickly.

"The middle of May."

Lord Jesus, just Your name is comfort. It's amazing what You can get us through, what the human spirit and body can endure. Thank You that You are all-sufficient when we are helpless and ignorant. I know that Your Word is all-powerful. Thank You for the Scripture that you gave Jerry to speak aloud. I'm going to put this memory back into Your hands. Nothing good can come from my analyzing it anymore. How I praise You for sparing our lives!

29 | THE VOICES

JERRY CAME HOME from the hospital on the fifth day after surgery. We went shopping for hats for him; they'd shaved his head for the operation. Friends we happened to meet couldn't believe how good Jerry looked, or that we were actually out shopping.

We held hands everywhere we went now. Jerry smiled almost constantly. But early mornings were hard for him. He would wake up crying. Within a few minutes, however, he'd confess his fear and self-pity as sin, ask God for forgiveness, receive almost instant relief, and then smile again. I couldn't seem to feel anything. Sometimes I envied Jerry because he could cry.

I grieved deeply, though; grieved as though he were already gone. I recalled a poem I'd written in high school. Only the first few lines came back, but they were enough to intensify my agony:

Spring came again this year . . .
I knew it would . . .
And yet I wondered how it could.
But it came all green and pink and white . . .
Bringing sweet perfume that spilled into the night.

I hadn't thought of that poem in almost twenty-nine years. Now it played over and over in my mind. My mind, in fact, was filled with voices over which I seemed to have no control.

I became almost physically sick every evening about six. That had been Jerry's coming-home time. I used to sit in a chair in the living room by the window and watch for his car. If I wasn't busy, sometimes I would watch for more than an hour—a habit I had formed in childhood when I watched for Mother to come home from work. Even when I wasn't by the window, I could hear the car over the other sounds in our noisy home. It didn't matter whether Jerry and I were on especially good terms; my heart would still leap when I heard his car turn into the driveway. The voice now insisted, *He won't be coming home anymore. What will you do?*

When we'd lived in Macon before the twins were born, Jerry got a promotion, which meant moving to Athens. He took a motel room there, intending to come home on weekends, while I was to remain in our Macon home with Julie and Jennifer until it sold. At six each evening I stood at the window in Macon believing somehow that he would come home even though I knew he was in Athens. When Jerry phoned every night, all I did was cry. After five days he came and got Julie and Jennifer and me. We moved into an old house in Athens and lived there until the Macon house sold and we could build a new one. I never complained; my husband was home in the evening.

Now, although Jerry was right there at home recuperating from his brain surgery, I would watch the clock for six to come. When it did, I was unable to keep from going to the living room window and looking out. *He's sitting down in the den*, I would try to reason with myself. *Why are you looking out the window?* The voices would reply, *You're trying to see what it will feel like when he isn't coming home anymore. You need to do this.*

So I looked out, watching, hurting, terrified of the cars moving past our house. They all had husbands in them. Then I went back and looked down the five steps from the kitchen to where Jerry was sitting on the sofa in the den. "See, he's right there," I would whisper to myself. "There's no need to look out the window."

Inevitably though, I would walk back to the window, my fear taking over. *There's no possible way I can live without him*, I told God again. *I can't live for my children, or to write. It's not enough. He's my world. I'm sorry. I know that's not right. But he is.*

It wasn't exactly like praying. God seemed far away. I was used to His being so close that I could almost touch Him. Now the terrifying voices seemed to be all I could hear.

I had to do all the driving now. And sometimes when I was alone in the car, the voices would show me a certain curve and point out, *If you went very fast around this curve, you could end it all. You could get relief. You know you can't live without him. Even if you weren't killed, you'd get to go to the hospital and they'd give you something and you wouldn't have to make decisions anymore.*

I always made myself slow down until I crept along the expressway with everyone passing me. But I would imagine myself speeding around the curve . . .

Thanksgiving came. Somehow I thought maybe it wouldn't this year. Our families came and cooked and brought food, and we did all the traditional things. I had lost fifteen pounds in the less-than-a-month since the tumor was discovered. I couldn't eat. I didn't think I would ever eat again, or even smile. Sometimes when I was out at the store, I'd look at women alone, wondering if they were widows, and I'd watch to see if they ever smiled.

Night after night I prayed for Jerry after he fell asleep. I would reach over and move my hand up and down his body, praying for total healing. Sometimes I prayed half the night. Other times I knelt beside him on the bed and prayed, or friends came in to pray with us. We confessed our sins, forgave each other, made everything right between us and everyone we knew.

But no matter what I did, or what Jerry did, each morning it was the same for me. Just as I was coming out of sleep, before I was even half-awake, the voices (there were always more in the morning) were waiting for me with a message that never changed: *Your husband is dying. Your husband is dying . . .*

Oh, God, help me. Please help me. Fear is eating me alive. I'm afraid to go to sleep and afraid to wake up. Send an answer of some kind, any kind. You have to help me get past this horrifying fear. Please.

30 | THE CHRISTMAS TREE

THERE WAS NOTHING I COULD DO to stop Christmas from coming. Jerry was to have that week off from radiation treatments.
After his last session before the holiday, the doctor gave him and
each of his patients a potted poinsettia plant to take home.
Outside the hospital in the cold air, Jerry wasn't sure where
the car was. He had trouble walking. I had to help him into the
passenger seat.

I couldn't buy presents. The children kept insisting that I go
Christmas shopping, or at least tell them what to buy. I just stared
through them as though I didn't understand what they were saying.

"Can we have a tree?" Jeremy asked.

"No," I almost shouted. "No tree. I won't ever have a tree in
this house again." So often Jerry and I had quarreled over the
Christmas tree . . .

One time when Julie was just a baby, he had insisted we go
out to the country and cut our own tree, like when he was a boy.
I had forgotten Julie's bottle and she was screaming as Jerry drove
slowly down a wooded lane. "We could have bought a tree for
what the ax cost," I grumbled. I grumbled a lot back then.
Suddenly he saw the one he wanted, parked the car, and got out.
He'd just been cutting a few minutes when an irate elderly man
appeared and informed us that this was all private property. So we
had a store-bought tree anyhow.

Jerry always wanted me to whip up soap powder and put it

on the tree to look like snow, as his mother had when he was a boy in Galax, Virginia. Jennifer had finally done it for him. He'd sat and looked at the result with tremendous satisfaction. "Now that's a tree!"

Now, this horrible Christmas, while I was out for a little at the grocery store, the children put up a tree. I wouldn't even look at the loathsome thing. A friend brought us new red placemats, very cheery. I finally managed to put them on the table, but it was as though they weighed a hundred pounds each. I hung our traditional wreath on the front door; even that simple action required energy and courage I didn't know I possessed.

I made countless trips to the drugstore to get prescriptions filled for Jerry. I would stand in line staring grimly ahead while people chatted and Christmas music filled the store. I had to walk past the gift wrap to the prescription counter, feeling as though I were walking on hot coals. I watched husbands hold open doors for wives whose arms were full of packages. I watched fathers talking to children and listened as women told each other what they were getting their husbands. I almost gasped with pain when I walked by the card counter and saw the section marked *Season's Greetings: Husbands.*

Christmas hit Jerry hard too. "Let's go for a ride, Mannie," he said one evening. We wrapped up and I got Jerry settled and then slid behind the wheel. I drove around and around. A steady, cold rain was falling. Even the windshield wipers seemed to insist, *You're scared. You're scared.* We looked at the lights in happy homes.

Then Jerry began to cry, quietly. I still couldn't cry. I just had a dry ache that was the deepest pain I'd ever known. Finally I pulled into a shopping center and parked. We watched people laughing, running, shopping while Jerry's muffled crying filled the car. Just four months ago—less than that, I thought—we were part of those people. Illness was totally foreign to us. Oh, God, why couldn't we go back? I'd never fuss again. I'd put soap on the tree.

I got out of the car and went into a drugstore and bought Jerry some mints. His mouth was always dry from the medicine he took. "Merry Christmas," the man said, giving me my change. I wanted to at least smile. I tried. But no smile came.

I drove to our home three times, and each time Jerry said, "I can't go in. Not yet." The fourth time he was smiling that wonderful smile we all depended on, and I turned into the driveway and cut the motor off.

The only shopping I'd done was to get sheets to fit the hospital bed we'd gotten for him. He wasn't using it yet, but we had it downstairs in our rec room, all set up for when he couldn't go up the stairs to our bedroom anymore.

It rained for three solid weeks that December. One morning we made a great effort and drove to church in the pouring rain. Just Jerry and me; the children stayed at home with their grandparents. On our carport were mounds of dead and dying worms. They always got swept onto the carport when we had too much rain. We had to step on some of them to get to the car. Suddenly I knew how they felt. I hadn't seen anything in this nightmare that I could identify with—except the worms.

I finally agreed to let the children get Christmas presents. They picked out a red and navy blue running suit for Jerry from me, and a doll for our granddaughter Jamie, Julie and Ricky's little girl. Jerry loved the running suit. He put it on and said, "Watch me, I'm going to do push-ups." He had barely been able to get into the suit. I was having to walk everywhere with him now. He'd fallen in the shower recently and cut his hand, and there'd been several other falls. I had safety bars put up in the bathroom and determined to watch him more closely. He never complained. Not once.

The doctor prescribed a brace for his left foot to keep it from dragging. He'd lost the use of his left hand completely. Still, he insisted on dressing himself, although it took him an hour. "I can do it," he'd tell me like a determined child.

I desperately wanted someone to hold on to emotionally. I couldn't lean on Jerry now. I knew I should lean on Jesus. Why wasn't I doing it?

You're a Christian, the voices mocked. *Where's your victory?*

I thought of the restoration formula that had always worked for me in the past: *No matter what is taken away from you, if you keep your eyes on Jesus and praise Him, He will restore it to you. You will be joyful to the exact degree you have hurt. What you have lost will be replaced—joy for mourning, beauty for ashes.*

That Christmas Eve, standing alone at the foot of the steps, I prayed, "God, I don't see how the restoration principle could possibly work now. I don't see how You'll ever come to me again in any shape or form. But I'm not going to limit You, so I'm going to remember this moment for the rest of my life. And if and when You restore the years that the locusts have eaten, I'll tell people about it. I'm committing to You to remember this agony, and if You can come up with some kind of joy equal to the I hurt I feel tonight, You are truly a God of miracles."

I turned to go up the seventeen steps to help Jerry get ready for bed. But then I looked back down into the den. The Christmas tree lights were still on. I hadn't looked directly at it since the children put it up. For twenty-four years, Jerry had always unplugged the Christmas tree lights each night. Always. I made myself walk over to the tree and looked at it for the very first time. I squinted like a little girl, trying to see how pretty I could make the lights, if I could make the tree look magical, wondrous.

Even when I squinted, the tree was not even close to beautiful. There was no beauty anywhere this Christmas.

Lord, I can barely pray. Nothing in me wants to pray. I want to curl up and die too. Life is losing its meaning. I have only the smallest glimmer of hope that You can somehow come through and make sense of all this. A part of me—a small part, true, but still a part of me— refuses to believe You've forgotten about me. I'm still on the lookout for You, somewhere, somehow.

BANISHING THE VOICES | 31

JERRY FACED HIS ILLNESS like a warrior—unafraid, even joking. But I was paralyzed by my fear of losing him. Fear kept me from sleeping, eating, thinking, praying, laughing, reasoning. I breathed fear rather than air, it seemed, and it lodged itself deep inside me.

I woke up one morning, having slept only in spurts and feeling as though an elephant sat on my chest. The familiar, silent voices chanted, *Your husband's dying . . .* As desperate as Jerry's situation was, I felt desperate too. How could I help and support him when there was no energy or faith left in me?

I started crying. It was the second time during Jerry's illness that tears had come. Mostly, I was too afraid to cry. "Help me," I finally asked Jerry. "Something is devouring me on the inside."

Jerry grabbed the Bible and began to pray for me. For a while we put his problem to one side in order to concentrate on mine. "Marion," Jerry said suddenly, "there's a word from your childhood that you need to say . . . a word you don't want to say. Just one word. Think. What is it? God wants to heal you of something."

Jerry never said things like this. We were faithful churchgoers, but this kind of thing he'd always thought was . . . well . . . weird. And anyhow, how would he know about such a word, unless God had told him? *Could God have spoken to my husband? Or is this simply more confused thinking due to his growing brain tumor?*

It must have been God, because right away I knew what the word was. I could see it very clearly, sitting solidly in my mind like a boulder. I'd never known I couldn't say this word before.

"Yes," I almost screamed.

"Say it!" Jerry commanded as we lay perfectly still.

"No."

"You have to, to get help."

"I can't."

He prayed, putting his hand on my head as I went through a fierce inner struggle. Jerry sat up and grabbed me by the shoulders, almost roughly, "Say the word."

"No!"

I could see it so clearly. It was on a greeting card that my mother must have fixed for me to give my daddy on Father's Day. I discovered the card after I was an adult and often looked at it—but simply would not ever say the word.

Jerry was crying now. "You have to, Mannie—in the Name of Jesus. You must be set free from fear. I need you free of fear."

The word moved to my mouth and sat there as surely as if I held a bite of food.

Jerry waited.

I opened my mouth and whispered as softly as possible, "Daddy."

"You never knew him, did you?"

I shook my head.

"Say it again."

"Daddy," I said a bit louder.

"He loved you."

"He left me."

I could see the greeting card clearly now. A little girl sitting up in her father's lap with his arms around her. The printed message read, "Happy Father's Day to my Daddy." The man and child were wearing clothes from the late 1930s. On the inside my mother had signed, "Love, Marion."

We got up and got dressed. All that morning, I said it over and over—"Daddy, Daddy." Gradually, amazingly, I discovered I could say it without fear or resentment or feelings of rejection. I told Jerry about the card, told him how I used to get it out and play with it and pretend my father was still alive. I even told him that when I played paper dolls with my friends, I'd pretend that their fathers were dead and mine was alive.

Something healed deep inside me, perhaps because God showed me clearly that I hadn't been abandoned, even though it *felt* as though I had when I was a child.

That afternoon two of my dearest friends came over. Dru, Caryl, and I ended up kneeling on the floor of our rec room. They prayed for a while, telling fear that it had to come out. Finally Caryl asked, "Marion, do you want to be fear-free?"

Shocked, I examined my feelings and discovered that I was afraid to let it go. Then I'd have to face the hard things in life and couldn't just back off or run away or hide myself in my fear. When I explained my feelings to my friends, Caryl smiled and said softly, "Well, you can hold on to fear if you want to. We have to be going now."

"No, wait," I begged. "I want to be fear-free!"

"Then you tell it to leave. Say it out loud like you mean it, like you hate it, like you've had enough."

Ignoring the mocking voice that said: *How silly. Are you really going to do this?* I said, "Fear, in the powerful Name of Jesus, you get out of me and my life. You go now—in Jesus' name!"

Right there with my eyes shut, I saw something in my spirit. I got a vivid picture of a stooped little man, all gray, wearing a ragged gray coat and a floppy gray hat. He was leaving, but looking back over his stooped shoulder with resentment and anger because he knew he had to go in the Name of Jesus. He simply couldn't stay any longer. I knew his name was fear and that he'd been living safely inside me for years.

Even though I didn't understand it, I knew it was real. Finally I stood up and took a deep breath. It was as if the pure clean fresh air had gone deep into my soul and everything was clean and fresh and pure all the way through me, down to my toes. There were ministering angels in that rec room. The next morning, I awakened to beautiful silence with Scripture marching through my mind. "I will never forsake you: I haven't given you a spirit of fear . . . Trust in the Lord with all your heart . . ." The chanting voices were no more.

Lord, You banished my fear when I called on Your name. But sometimes now I can feel fear peering at me from the corner of my room, looking for a way back in. Help me to remember that it's powerless against me, that Your perfect love casts out all fear.

PART EIGHT

"I WILL REJOICE IN THE GOD OF MY SALVATION"

32 | ONE SIMPLE WORD FROM GOD

By MARCH, Jerry, who'd never had a headache in his life before the tumor or missed a day's work in almost twenty-five years, began having horrific headaches. I chased after every cancer treatment I heard of. I read about a new "wonder drug" and got some of it shipped to us. In a medical report Jerry's physician wrote, "The patient's wife is phoning medical centers all over the country. She is, of course, desperate."

That desperation, had I but known it, meant I was on the royal highway to something I began calling Nevertheless Living. Translated, that meant that no matter what happens—even brain cancer—God is not a God of "what if"; He is a God of "nevertheless." I began searching through my Bible and found two hundred Scriptures about *nevertheless*. Many of them showed that, despite expected failure, success was possible! I became obsessed with the word, and I was certain God had given it to me.

"Then they were very wroth, And conspired all of them together to come and to fight against Jerusalem. . . . *Nevertheless* we made our prayer unto our God" (Nehemiah 4:7–9).

"For I said in my haste, I am cut off from before thine eyes: *nevertheless* thou heardest the voice of my supplications when I cried unto thee" (Psalm 31:22).

"So foolish was I, and ignorant: I was as a beast before thee. *Nevertheless* I am continually with thee" (Psalm 73:22–23).

"*Nevertheless* my lovingkindness will I not utterly take from him, nor suffer my faithfulness to fail" (Psalm 89:33).

Simon's response when Jesus instructs him to launch out into the deep: "Master, we have toiled all the night, and have taken nothing: *nevertheless* at thy word I will let down the net" (Luke 5:5).

Jesus' response when the Pharisees warn Him that Herod is determined to kill him: "*Nevertheless* I must walk today, and tomorrow" (Luke 13:33).

"I am crucified with Christ: *nevertheless* I live . . . by the faith of the Son of God, who loved me, and gave himself for me" (Galatians 2:20).

Nevertheless became as real to me as the people I saw every day. It was even a tiny, but powerful sentence: Never the *less*. But always the *most* with God. When the voices accused me and woke me up early, I tried out the new word. *Nevertheless, you may notice that I'm not afraid!* I'd whisper in all kinds of situations. Sometimes I'd shout the words driving in the car alone on an errand for Jerry. Fear would be after me hard and fast, but I'd cling to the words—especially *that* word and the power behind it. Fear hated the nevertheless principle and backed down like a coward.

One day when God was telling me about the victorious life that I'd lead one day, fear intruded with: *You're crazy, Marion. You've finally flipped under all the pressure. It's to be expected.*

Quicker than John Wayne could whip out his gun, I shot back with, "Nevertheless, fear, you may notice that I'm not afraid. That's joy in my heart!"

No response from fear.

God seemed to continue speaking. *You have another life to live. I am in control. There's something you have to do. I have chosen you very carefully. You can't understand now; it's too soon. Just trust. With every breath you take, trust Me. No matter what happens, You're going to be fine. Your days of fear are finally over. You've been afraid all of your life. It's possible to live fear-free, Marion.*

Fear tried to suggest, *Marion, what kind of a God would take your husband at forty-seven and leave you alone with children to raise?* Somewhere I'd read that we have eight seconds to refuse a thought. That's all.

I was alone, so I spoke out loud. "I want to tell you, Father, that I fully realize no one is taking Jerry from me. I give him to You. I let go. It almost feels like . . . worship. It's not my battle."

It never was, but I had to let you wear yourself out and come to Me beaten and all out of ideas before I could hold you and reassure you. You held on for so long. Many dear children never let go. They hold on for a lifetime, even after someone is gone. This earthly existence is like a play. Each one is assigned a part with the proper entrances and exits. You are just in the play. For a long time you were trying to direct it.

"You're so much bigger than I knew. Who would ever have thought that I could let go and have all this joy too?"

I suddenly remembered once burning my hand very badly. The only relief I found was to stand at the faucet and let the cold water stream over it. Now Jesus, the Living Water, was giving me relief, and I couldn't bear to move away. My mind and spirit and body were all standing at the stream. Never mind the circumstances. God was not limited by circumstances.

He is the God of Nevertheless. I can't lose! "Whatever You choose is fine with me, Father," I went on, "I'm not trying to direct the play anymore. I am fully convinced that You are bringing about something marvelous and that Jerry and I will both continue to live in victory, even if we aren't together. I don't understand this, but I do believe. No one will understand my joy, but I don't care. It's real."

Don't talk about it yet. Just ponder it for a while. The time will come when you can share it. Now is not the time. I am going to use all of this. Nothing will be wasted. Trust Me. I have something for you to do. No one else can do it. Don't indulge in any self-pity whatsoever or I cannot use you.

"I won't, Father. Use me in any way You want to. I long to be a vessel. That used to be a scary thought, You know." I well remembered hearing a lovely widow speaking about being a vessel for the Lord. I had told Him right then, "God, I will not be a vessel. I will only be a wife. You *have* to let Jerry live."

The enemy, fear, had totally convinced me that my life, and certainly my joy, was over. He had me believing I would live like a zombie—if I chose to continue living.

And in that condition of total defeat, when I had no will to go on fighting, I had somehow stumbled into Nevertheless Living.

My total relinquishment of Jerry and my first steps in Nevertheless Living had come on May 11, 1983. In order to go on living, I had to die to every dream, every right, every ambition. My life had to begin again. My neat little mapped-out future of growing old with Jerry had to be erased like a blackboard at the end of a school day. It was a tremendous price to pay for peace and joy, but it was the only way to be fear-free. Now I felt as though I were drifting down a lazy river with my hand hanging over the side of a boat. I'd go wherever the gentle river took me. No more struggling to go upstream against the current.

Jerry's funeral on July 19, 1983, wasn't nearly as difficult as the mocking voices of fear had been. I was fully convinced that God had not taken my husband. Rather, He had received him—with love.

After his death early on a Sunday morning, I fell into bed around 3:30 A.M. My dear oncology nurse friend, Rose McKeever, who had been Jerry's at-home nurse, spent the rest of the night with me. Julie had come from her home to sleep over. She and Jennifer were in Jen's room and, of course, Jon and Jeremy, now fifteen, were in theirs. My mother was also with us.

Once we were in bed, Rose said, "Are you asleep, Marion?"

"No. It's all been so . . . marvelous. Knowing Jerry's well now, able to move again, to run. He's well, Rose. I think I'm excited."

"Me too! But what's that music I hear?"

We'd kept music—praise music—playing for the last six weeks in the hospital room we'd set up for Jerry in our rec room downstairs. He had requested it. "I turned the music off," I said.

"Are you sure?" Rose sat up in bed.

"I'm sure."

Just then, Julie tiptoed into our room, "Mother, what's that music we hear?"

"I don't know. Rose and I hear it too."

Julie went back to bed and Rose went to sleep, but I listened and listened. *What is it, Lord? Will You tell me?* I fully expected Him to, for some reason. The music sounded like thousands of soft voices. You had to listen to hear them. The words were lovely, like jewels of sound, but they were in a language I didn't know. I thought they might be Hebrew. I decided to concentrate on one word and memorize it. They were all so lovely, but I finally chose one that I kept hearing over and over. It sounded like *sone-yah*. I whispered the word to myself. Somehow it satisfied me deeply.

Marion, Jerry's home now. This is a welcome-home song we are singing to him. He's in the center of the singers. He's fine. Finer than he's ever been.

I gasped and laughed at the same time. Afterward, I carried the word around with me like a beautiful stone you'd slip into your pocket.

It was several years before I found a translation. I'd asked a host of people about the word—the only one I'd selected from so many. No one knew. Perhaps I wasn't pronouncing it correctly. Then one day when I was buying a pair of shoes with Jennifer, she nodded toward the shoe salesman and said, "Mom, maybe he knows about your word. Ask him." The young man, newly arrived in America from Jerusalem, seemed to be waiting for me to ask him.

"I'd like to ask you about a word I think might be Hebrew," I said to him.

"What word?"

"It's something like *sone-yah*."

He smiled. "Ah! How can I explain it to you? Let's see. . . . If there were a beautiful garden and I were to select only one flower for you, I'd pick the most wonderful one, of course."

I nodded.

"That flower would be a *sone-yah*. The best."

I blinked happy tears away and paid for my shoes.

Father God, why has it taken me so long, why did I have to struggle so hard to come to a place of surrender? I wish I could have done it sooner, trusted You sooner, been stronger, braver. I feel like crumpled paper. It's as if a terrible pain has suddenly ceased. Thank You for this wonderful place of rest in You.

FEEDING THE FEW | 33

"Where's breakfast, Mom?" Jon bellowed up the stairs to me. "Other mothers get up in the morning and cook breakfast!"

"Well, I'm not other mothers!" I yelled back, pulling the covers up to my chin. I'd hated cooking breakfast, even when Jerry was alive, but I'd done it. Now I just didn't make the effort. By my second year of being a widow, I was having a hard time being in the kitchen. We ate out a lot, or I made sandwiches. When we gathered around the kitchen table, our family looked so much smaller. Julie had been married for some years and was expecting her second child. And Jennifer had married Charlie Van Pelt. We used to be six; now we were only three. I tried not to think about the day when Jon and Jeremy, now almost sixteen, would be gone too.

My relationship with Jon and Jeremy was poor in other areas too. They resented my being their only parent. Sometimes I resented it myself. Being the final authority was hard.

"You're too strict. Daddy was never like this," Jeremy complained one day. He was almost crying. Jon chimed in. "Yeah, if you don't give me more freedom, I'm moving out when I'm nineteen."

"You're moving out at sixteen if you don't watch your mouth," I blurted out. I didn't mean it, but I didn't want them to run all over me.

One morning after a breakfast of cereal, the boys saw me moving chairs down into the den. "Are you having that stupid Bible study here again?" Jeremy asked.

"You know it's not stupid! People get help here."

"Good for them. *We* don't. You never have time for us anymore. You're always doing thing for other people, Mama—even strangers."

There was a lot of truth in that statement but I chose to ignore it. "Help me move the chairs," I said.

"Why can't your good Christian friends help you?" Jeremy asked.

I made him move the chairs, but as he left, he said, "I know there won't be any supper tonight. There never is when you have your big-deal Bible study."

So we were back to arguing about food. One evening Jeremy said, honestly and without apparent anger, "Won't we ever come home from school and smell supper cooking again and sit around the table and be a family?"

Oh, how I wanted to tell him that we would. I should have been able to do that. *What mother doesn't cook?*

I continued to have the Bible study. I also attended other prayer meetings and Bible studies and got involved with helping people. Sometimes the boys would come home and a stranger and I would be sitting at the kitchen table, talking or praying. After the company left, Jeremy would ask, "Why can't they go somewhere else for help?"

"You know I like being involved with people and helping them."

"Me and Jon are people. You don't do much for us . . ."

"That's not true, Jeremy. Anyway, I have to have some kind of life besides cooking and puttering around the house and saying hello and good-bye to you two. I can't just cling to you boys. One day . . ."

I finished the sentence in my mind. *You two will be gone also. I'll be alone.* I've never wanted to be alone.

Another voice spoke in my thoughts. I knew Whose it was. *Are you leaving the boys before they leave you? They really need you now. I can handle your future.*

My reaction to that suggestion was to attack the oven with a powerful cleanser and make a mental list of people who'd been helped at my Bible study.

In December of 1984 I decided to go on a mission trip to the slums of the Philippines. Jon and Jeremy didn't want me to go.

"What if you don't come back?" Jeremy asked quietly.

"Then we'll know they made missionary stew out of Mom," Jon said.

"Jonnnnn!" Jeremy hollered. Jon laughed, but I saw the concern beneath his joke.

I arranged for a trusted couple to move in and stay with the boys. Just as I was about to leave for the airport, a phone call from their school informed me that Jeremy was in trouble again and would be suspended for two days for using inappropriate language. I made a quick trip to school. I had seldom seen Jeremy so upset; I hated leaving him like that, but go I did.

I phoned home from the Philippines several times. "I'm learning so much, Jeremy," I told him. "You'll probably have a new mom when I get back home."

"I don't want a new mom," Jeremy said. "I just want my old one. Come back home *now*—please."

I tried to sound cheerful and reassuring. "Guess what? Yesterday I fed about three hundred hungry children breakfast and told them about Jesus." There was no response.

It was nearly Christmas when my plane landed in Atlanta. Jeremy and Jon met me at the airport, accompanied by the couple who'd stayed with them while I was gone. Jeremy pushed his way through the people meeting the plane, and we held each other for a long time. "I thought you wouldn't come back," he whispered.

At the house, he showed me the tree he had bought and decorated himself. "Sit down at the table, Mama. I'll make you a bowl of tomato soup," he announced.

The kitchen was warm, homey, and comfortable. Jeremy watched as I ate the soup as though it were a gourmet dinner. For some reason, two tears slipped right into it. I was startled and confused. Since just before Jerry had died, I'd been unable to cry about anything. My tears seemed trapped deep inside me. Yet now two went *plop, plop* right into my soup.

In January, Jeremy mentioned that Jon was getting pretty good at basketball. He played on the school team. "They're in a tournament now, Mom. Most all of the parents come to the games."

Jeremy knew I liked basketball about as much as cooking breakfast. Of course, when Jerry had been alive, I had attended all the boys' games. Jerry had insisted that I go. He was the most enthusiastic parent at any ballgame. One time he even flew home early from a business trip to see a football game. He was always in the stands cheering. I hadn't been to any kind of a game since he'd been gone. I hadn't even asked who'd won.

One morning about five o'clock, God seemed to be speaking to me. *There is a reason why your boys keep getting into trouble. They are becoming more and more rebellious because they have a rebellious mother.*

I sat up straight in bed, fully awake, and whispered back to Him as the first light of the new day entered the room. "What? Look at all I'm doing for You."

Then God gave me some instructions that I didn't like or understand at all. *Go to Jon's game this Friday night.*

"Go to a basketball game instead of a dynamic Bible study? It's not logical—or even spiritual."

I didn't want to go to that basketball game at all. I don't like noise or sports. Feeling rather foolish, I called off the Bible study and went to the game.

Jon's school was losing by seventeen points at halftime. Suddenly Jon began to make basket after basket. He scored thirty points, and in the last two minutes of the game, his team won! I was on my feet screaming, clapping, cheering.

I went back the next night for the second game of the tournament. On the final night, award presentations were scheduled, and at the last minute I went. The announcer called out boys' names for awards. Finally he said, "And now the award for the most valuable player of the year, voted on by all the coaches in the tournament—Jon West."

The applause was deafening. I sat motionless, stunned. As the crowd rose to its feet cheering, I thought, *I almost didn't come. I could have missed this.* My vision blurred. The salty tears tasted wonderful. I clapped till my hands hurt.

On the way home, Jon held his plaque quietly. Finally he spoke. "Daddy would have been proud of me. He'd have smiled all the way home. The men at his office would have had to hear about the game tomorrow. And we'd have talked about every play when we got home tonight, ya know?"

I swallowed hard. "Yes, Jon, I know."

"Hey, Mom, did you feel a little proud of me? That I was your son? I mean, did you clap or anything? Are you glad I'm not a nerd or something? They say I might get a scholarship. You think God could swing that?"

"Oh yes, I'm sure He could. And it's so much fun being your

mother. I had no idea you were so good. I'm terribly proud of you. And I'm coming to your baseball games when they start."

I discontinued the Bible studies in my home and decided that I couldn't make the return trip to the Philippines that the mission group was planning. I tried to be at home every day when the boys got in from school. I began learning to listen, and we started talking more. Jeremy didn't get a single demerit at school that semester, and Jon didn't mention moving out again.

Of course, they weren't perfect, but their response to me was different. Once I confronted Jon about something; both of us were expecting me to give him the lecture of the century. But suddenly, as I looked at him, unexpected words burst out. "Oh, Jon, I love you so much. I don't want you to get into trouble. I know it's hard for you to make the right decisions, but I want you to turn out okay more than anything in the world. I know I haven't done everything right since Daddy's been gone—I've made some big mistakes, but please know that I love you."

He grabbed me, all six feet two inches of him, in a bear hug. "I love you too, Mama. I'm sorry about what I did. I was wrong. I know it was wrong. Go ahead and punish me. I really want to do what's right. You're a good mom. Just keep on saying 'no' and loving us, and we're going to be okay—all of us."

A while later, I popped out of bed early one morning with a strange new desire. I went to the kitchen and made oatmeal, bacon, toast, and hot chocolate for the boys. Standing at the stove stirring the thick oatmeal, I started crying. *God, what is this? No one cries over oatmeal.* But I felt wonderful, happy, secure, excited—obedient, no longer in rebellion.

Then a picture came clearly to my mind: I was feeding three hundred hungry children in the Philippines—feeding them breakfast and telling them about Jesus. *Oh, Lord, I do see. I have to start at home, don't I? With my own children. Never mind that one day they'll leave too.* I poured out the oatmeal, and God poured such joy into me that I thought I might do cartwheels right across the floor. But I knew the boys wouldn't understand, so I settled for humming "Amazing Grace."

They came into the kitchen sniffing the aromas of breakfast, and Jeremy said, "Hey, Jon, she even made our lunch!"

Father, You know how much I didn't want to be a widow. Nevertheless, I was one. I needed You to be my husband and Jon's and Jeremy's father. Some things that I thought were so right, turned out all wrong. Show me, guide me, help me be the mother they need.

34 | MAKING SMALL TALK

BE FIRM AND LOVE THEM and cook a lot. I tried to convince myself that that was all I needed to do to be a good mom to my boys. But they still deceived me, lied to me, came in after curfew. Once I locked Jon outside when he came home drunk. He curled up with our collie in the backyard and slept soundly. I spent most of the night watching him from the upstairs window.

Jeremy seemed to turn into a workaholic—he kept the yard in perfect shape and took a part-time job. Although he had an explosive temper, he didn't stay angry for long. Jon was quiet, keeping his feelings to himself. After graduating from high school, Jeremy chose to stay at home and work. He had a knack for putting money away and wanted to start his own landscaping business.

Jon, on the other hand, went to college. *Good,* I thought, *maybe he'll find himself there.* Then I received his grades for the first semester: He was failing or barely passing all subjects. I got him on the telephone and chewed him out.

"Cool it, Mom. You worry too much," he said. "I'll pull my grades up." Everything was always future tense with Jon.

"Are you partying?" I demanded.

"Mom, stop grilling me."

"Are you happy? Do you go to church? Do you read your Bible?"

"Mom, can't you just make small talk?" There was anger in his voice and his usual charm was gone. The line went dead.

Toward the end of the second semester, when the only things Jon was doing well were playing tennis and partying, I pulled him out of school.

Back home, Jon and I fought over almost everything. He broke every rule I made. I screamed, nagged, bribed, pouted and cried. One evening during a heated argument, when I wanted to know more about a party he was going to, I became so angry I grabbed the keys to his beloved green truck and threw them into a field behind the house. After screaming at me, he went to look for the keys. Sometime later I heard his truck roar out of the driveway.

At two in the morning he still hadn't come home. I stood staring out the window, willing his truck to come around the corner. "God," I prayed, "send Jon home." *If he were a little boy, he'd be asleep in bed,* I thought. *I could slip into his room and kiss him good night.*

Tired of waiting, I went down to the kitchen and discovered Jon hadn't taken out the trash. I tied up the bag and took it outside. There by the trashcan I heard the rumble of Jon's green truck. *Thank You, God.* Jon slowed down, cut the lights and engine, and glided soundlessly into the driveway. He slipped out of the truck, leaving the door ajar. I wanted to rush up and hug him, but halfway there I could smell the drink on his breath. I refused to let him in the house.

He spent another night curled up with the dog out back, snoring loudly. At eight the next morning, I unlocked the door. What had I proven?

I wanted Jon to go to counseling with me, but he wouldn't stick with it. I arranged for an off-duty policeman to "happen by" and shoot baskets with him. I handpicked young people and suggested ways they could influence Jon's life for the better. I bought books, pamphlets and tapes for him.

Once I found out that Jon was at a party at a friend's house with no parents home. I rang the doorbell of the lovely home and asked the girl who answered if Jon was there. She said he wasn't; I went in anyway. Young people began ducking and hiding there. "It's Mrs. West!" someone hollered. I opened the pantry door in the kitchen and found Jon hiding. "Let's go *home*," he said, his fists and jaw clenched,

In our driveway he stepped out of the car and pounded his fist against the drainpipe of our house, almost flattening it, then casually wiped his bleeding hand on his jeans.

Another time, after an argument, he walked into his room, where I heard a loud thud. When I went to check on him, he was looking at a huge gaping hole he'd punched in the wall. The next day I made him repair the wall, and I hung a nice picture over it. But nothing could repair the hole in my heart.

Each day brought a new fight with Jon. People called him at three in the morning. Many times I simply left the phone off the hook.

By now I knew Jon was drinking, smoking pot, and involved with girls. One night I came downstairs when I heard him in the kitchen. "What are you doing?" I asked. It was past midnight.

"Just getting some water, Mom. Cool it. You always think the worst."

He set the full glass down and turned to close the refrigerator. I picked up the glass and took a long drink.

"Mom! Watch out! That's hundred-proof vodka!"

I coughed and spit most of it out, then poured the rest down the drain, stared coldly at Jon, and went upstairs. I'd tried everything I knew to make him straighten up.

A week later, he said, "Mother, you've been a widow nearly

four years. Why don't you go to the singles meeting at Yellow River Baptist Church? They're having a covered-dish dinner for singles. Make that asparagus casserole and go." Jon's answer to life's problems was food.

"No."

"Why not?"

"I'm shy. I don't want to do that. I'm almost fifty."

"I'll walk in with you if you'll go. Please."

I loved hearing him say please. But I knew he only wanted me out of the house more so he could have people over and not get caught. He wanted me to go out at night and stay out a long time.

"I'm not going. Besides, I don't want to date. I would like to be a . . . wife again." I surprised myself by saying that. But it was true. I had loved being married.

"Well, Mom, what do you plan to do? Just sit here at the kitchen table and wait for the doorbell to ring and when you open it, there'll be your handsome, Spirit-filled husband-to-be—sent to you directly by God?"

I looked at Jon. "Maybe," I smiled.

"Mom, be sensible. You have to make the asparagus casserole and go to Yellow River Baptist Church. It's the only way."

"Jon, I like your idea of God sending someone to me. I think God can do it."

"Aw, Mom." He banged the table with his fist and got up to check out what was in the refrigerator.

I knew in my heart I was going to make a list of the qualities I wanted in a husband and ask God to select him for me. No dating—just marriage again with the man of God's choice.

By now Jon was working fulltime back at the butcher shop where he'd worked when he was in high school. He looked so wonderful standing behind the counter, smiling, saying, "Yes, ma'am," to the women customers and laughing. He was so polite and handsome! I'd go in and buy meat I didn't really need just to have a conversation with him some days. His eyes always said: *Mom, don't do anything weird, please.*

One day I phone him at work, "Are you busy, Jon?"

"No. What is it?"

"I was wondering, do you have any goals in life? Any real friends? Do you—"

The line went dead. Why had I done that? I knew Jon wanted me to learn to make small talk. Could that be too hard? Couldn't I do that for him? "Lord, I've failed with Jon. Jeremy too, I guess. I don't know how to help them. I've done so much wrong. I don't even know how to make small talk with my son. Make me teachable—let me be fun some of the time for them."

I sat down at the kitchen table and these thoughts came slowly but directly into my mind: *Your nagging and lack of trust are as bad as anything Jon has done. Let him go, Marion. For always. Give Jon to Me. Jeremy too. Trust Me with them. Do it now.*

How? How? How do I give a son—two sons to You? How do I know You'll . . . I'm sorry, Lord. Why can't I trust You? I want to please You and be the kind of mother Jon and Jeremy need. I think they would have been better off if their daddy had lived and I'd died.

Self-pity had snuck up on me. *No,* I decided. *I can't give in to that. Anxiety and self-pity are never from God.*

I began to think of all of Jon's good characteristics: how gentle he was with animals; the patient way he grilled steaks for all of us, making sure he got them exactly the way we wanted them; his sharp, dry sense of humor; his skill as a basketball player. I liked the way he cared about those shunned by others—a hearing-impaired young man, a lady with Down syndrome. Down deep, he was sensitive. Once at a family gathering, when my feelings got hurt and no one noticed, Jon quietly came over, put his arm around me, and gave me a hard, quick hug. Then he was gone.

I found a picture of Jon and Jeremy when they were only four, dressed in sailor suits and red shoes. Jon had hated those red shoes and fought with the shoe salesman when he had to try them on. "I hate 'em, Mom," he wailed. But I had my mind set on red shoes. I taped the eight-by-ten picture to the wall of my closet. Every time I went into my closet I thanked God for caring for Jon and Jeremy.

The next day, when Jon phoned from a friend's house asking to spend the night, I tried to make small talk. I said something about the Georgia Bulldogs football team that his father had so loved. I mentioned a new way I was cooking a roast.

"Hey, Mom, you're learning to make small talk. Good going!" I could feel him smiling. I wanted to stay connected to him—any way I could. A long time after we hung up, I just sat there holding the phone, remembering our "normal" conversation.

Father, You are so faithful even with my smallest request. You knew how much I wanted to learn to make small talk with Jon. It didn't come easily to me. But You continued to help me be a single mother. Show me more about small talk and having fun and not being so serious.

35 | RISING UP OVER DEPRESSION

IN ORDER TO HAVE some type of routine in our lives, I decided to apply for a position that I saw advertised in our church paper. It was a job at the counseling center at our church in downtown Atlanta. Never mind that I was phobic about driving back and forth to downtown Atlanta in bumper-to-bumper rush hour traffic; I needed to think about something besides myself. My secretarial skills weren't too good—I hadn't had a job outside the home since I'd been married. But I'd been a business major in college, because my mother had wanted me to know how to do something to support myself should I ever have needed to.

To my amazement I got the job. And I was a disaster—I made one mistake after another. I had the feeling everyone would be relieved if I quit—including me. But there was one good thing about the job: I began to take an interest in the people who came in for counseling. I prayed for them silently behind my desk and rejoiced over their progress as they showed up week after week.

I was exhausted when I got home, but I was content. Sleep came again, and so did laughter. I began to look forward to the next day. After several months I began to understand a little why God had wanted me to take the job. Doing something difficult—something for which I wasn't even qualified—had helped me because I was helping other people.

And I learned some things about depression: You can't escape it by running away; it's not just a woman's problem—it can attack men and even children; if depression persists, it's wise to seek professional help. But I also learned there were things I could do on my own to confront depression. I wrote them down in a little article I sent to *Guideposts* magazine:

1. *Arm yourself for the battle.* I read encouraging passages of Scripture and try to memorize them. (Isaiah 40:31 or 61:3, or Psalm 34:17, for instance.) I also read from a favorite book, *My Utmost for His Highest*, by Oswald Chambers. Or I listen to inspirational music, sometimes singing along. Of course, I don't *feel* like turning on the radio or tape player. But this is a battle.

2. *Try to pinpoint why you are depressed.* For instance, I miss being a wife, and I think that if I were a wife again, I wouldn't be depressed. But I must remember that I was a wife for twenty-five years, and there were often times when I felt depressed then. I explain to myself that people, circumstances and things don't make one really happy. Joy comes from choosing to believe that God is working in my life in *all* circumstances.

3. *Do something for someone else.* Dr. Karl Menninger of the famous Menninger Clinic once said there's one sure way to avoid having a breakdown, a solution so simple that almost no one will believe it works. You simply walk out your front door and find someone—anyone—who needs help, and you help him or her. Reaching out, reminding ourselves that we're not alone, is the first step back. We may not be immune from ever feeling depressed, but our powerful God is always standing ready to help us fight the battle against it. After all, He promised us that "sorrow and mourning shall flee away" (Isaiah 51:11).

Unknown to me, a sociology professor/minister/farmer in Oklahoma who'd just lost his wife of twenty-five years read that little article in *Guideposts*. He was so depressed that he could only read a small article. While reading it, he thought he heard from God. While he absorbed the article and wondered if he'd really heard from God, back in Georgia I was having one of the most horrible nights of my life.

I'd paid a man to fix a leak underneath the crawl space of our house. He'd charged me five thousand dollars, but the leak was still there. It was raining hard, and the water was about to spill over a retaining wall into our den and rec room. Wearing Jerry's old rubber boots, I sat under the house in the red Georgia mud with a borrowed sump pump. It wasn't enough.

Jeremy had helped me most of the day, but then the man who'd supposedly fixed the problem came by. "Too bad, lady. It ain't my fault," he said, preparing to leave. Profanity rolled from Jeremy's mouth and rage from his eyes. I stepped in between them and asked the man to leave. As he hurried out, Jeremy tried to follow, still screaming threats. When the man was gone, Jeremy stormed out.

Jon was supposed to be home from a camping trip, but he'd called and said he'd be staying longer. I knew there was more than camping going on.

I'd never felt more alone and helpless. The crawl space was dark, and only about four feet high. My legs were cramping terribly, and I was afraid.

Bone-weary, I began to listen to the enemy who seemed to be squatting in the mud with me. *Poor you. No one wants to help you. It's going to be this way the rest of your life, you know. You're going to be alone forever with problems like this—not to mention your sons*

and what they are doing. Why do you think God cares about you?
Why should He?

I had no hope left, none at all. I was as beaten as I'd been at any time during the last five years. I was almost convinced that God really didn't care, that He wasn't working all things for good for me.

Almost.

Then I did one of the hardest things I'd ever done: I climbed out from under the house and made myself dial some good friends down the street. My mouth went dry and my hands shook. I was terrified. *What if they're not at home? What if I'm intruding? What if they don't want to be with me?*

"Hello," Becky Martin answered. She always had the most wonderful hello of anyone I knew—bright, cheery, welcoming. She said hello like my mother had when she answered the phone at the Granite City Bank in Elberton.

"Becky—Becky—I—"

"Marion! Oh, hello. We were just talking about you. Rois and I. How are you?"

"Becky, I have to ask you something." I shut my eyes hard and took a deep breath. "If y'all are going anywhere tonight, let me go with you. It doesn't matter where. I just have to get away from this house for tonight and . . ."

"Oh, Marion!" her voice was overflowing with excitement. "We're going to eat out in Tucker, at the steak house. We'll pick you up in, say, thirty minutes, okay? This is wonderful!"

I hung up the phone and opened my eyes. *Thank You, Lord. You are still there, and You still care about me.*

Someone recommended a repairman who dropped everything and came to my house the next day. He was the president of a large company. He fixed the problem for five hundred dollars and advised me to call my insurance company about the water standing in our living room and rec room.

By now I felt human again. I thanked the man from the bottom of my heart and made the call to our insurance people. They came out immediately and were wonderful. New carpet was laid that week.

Three weeks later, on April 18, 1987, the professor/minister/ farmer from Oklahoma phoned, and with that one phone call my life was changed forever. When Gene Acuff wrote me a note later thanking me for talking with him, he signed the brief note, "Goodnight, Gene."

A cold chill ran all over me. Either I thought or God said: *One day he'll be telling you goodnight for the rest of your life, and it won't be over a phone. He's going to be your husband.*

We were married four months later.

Lord God, looking back, I know You sat in the mud under that crawl space with me. You gave me the courage to call Becky, to ask for help. Why is it so hard to ask for help? Keep pride out of my life; it creeps back in like a thief in the night.

PART NINE

"The Lord God Is My Strength, and He Has Made My Feet Like Hinds' Feet..."

36 | PRAYER BOWLS AND OVERSHADOWING

JEREMY HAD BEEN LIVING in his new apartment for nearly a year. He missed Julie when she and Ricky and their family moved off to the new log house they'd built near Gene and me. But they stayed in touch by phone and saw each other, though not as often. They'd lived close by before their move, and anytime Jeremy stopped by, Julie gave him a good meal and tons of encouragement.

Then one day our phone rang; the caller ID said that it was Jeremy's number. I answered quickly.

"Hi, Jeremy." He sounded strange, but then his bipolar medications had made him less animated than he'd been for so long.

"It's Jon."

Silence.

"Oh, Jon . . . hey." None of the family knew exactly where Jon was living. We only knew for certain that he needed to return to Dunklin.

He'd been away from the program for more than two years and as they explained at Dunklin, "If guys 'fall again' after completing the program, they fall much deeper into addiction than they were when they entered the program."

Jon was in that much deeper place. The way drugs deceive a person, I decided, is that they don't know they are deceived. Our entire family was praying that Jon would decide he needed

Dunklin, become desperate and return. My standing offer remained: "When you are desperate, I'll get you to Dunklin. But I love you too much to help you continue your life as you're living it."

Once he'd said, "Maybe I'll just go on to heaven and play golf with Daddy. I look forward to heaven."

More silence from me. *God, I can't buy into fear now or I'll sink. Help me be strong and respond properly. It's not really Jon I'm talking with now, it's the addictions. We all want the real Jon back.*

I was disappointed that he'd managed to get into Jeremy's life and apartment. Jeremy was trying to avoid him because—unlike Gene and me, Julie and Ricky, Jennifer and Charlie—he found it almost impossible to say no to Jon. "He's my brother," he'd told me painfully. "We were in the womb together."

I'd nodded. More and more I responded with silence or a nod. Time was when I could respond to any comment, good or negative, with a long speech.

So Jeremy gave him money or let him sleep on the floor in his one-bedroom apartment. But he hated doing it, knowing it wasn't good for Jon, wasn't bringing him to the point of desperation. Sometimes he couldn't make him leave, and one of them would phone and Jon would be very close to losing his temper. Jeremy rarely lost his temper now.

Jon's voice on the phone was sometimes very low, sometimes loud and angry; he'd argue theology, only the addictions twisted the truth. Sometimes almost nothing he said made sense. Often he hung up abruptly. He didn't want to hear anything I had to say. It was all about him and his needs.

"I'm going back to Dunklin," he said quietly one night.

How many people were praying for that? It was impossible to

know. Even some of the guys at Dunklin were praying Jon back, I'd heard. Then why wasn't I jumping up and down? Why was my heart heavy? Why didn't I believe him?

Because he was lying.

"So come and pick me up at Jeremy's."

"Can't do that, Jon."

"What? Why not?"

"You aren't serious."

"I don't have anywhere to live! Jeremy's not going to let me stay here any longer. I can't just stand out in the rain hungry, Mom. We're family."

Silence.

"You always have lots of things to say on the phone. Remember how you used to talk and ask me questions and give me ideas?"

Silence.

"I *know* you remember! What's wrong with you, anyway? Come and get me."

He was an hour and a half away. "I can't, Jon. I'm not going to play ball with you until you mean it. Until you are desperate."

I knew he'd sold everything he had for a fraction of its real value, even his beloved golf clubs. He had nothing but pride.

"Why don't you believe me, Mom?"

I took a deep breath and said softly, "You lie."

"When have I ever lied—just name once."

Oh, Jon, I can't remember truth coming out of your mouth since you were at Dunklin. If your mouth's moving, you're lying.

"Well, you lied when you phoned two weeks ago from Jeremy's and said you wanted to go to Dunklin."

"How was I lying?"

"By saying you wanted to go. Remember, I had you call

Dunklin and ask to be readmitted, and they were going to return your call." That's the way it works; the man wanting into the program must call himself. It's impossible to get someone on the phone who can say yes, so callers are phoned back. Always. "You waited three hours for the call. In the meantime a 'friend' was coming by Jeremy's to pick you up. While you were still waiting for him, the call came and Jeremy chased you around outside trying to get you to take the call. You didn't. Something more important than getting help came up."

The line went dead.

Everything in me screamed: *Give up on him!* I made myself get up and go to the refrigerator and stare at the beautiful picture we'd taken of Jon at Dunklin on the Fourth of July two years ago. He'd just won some kind of medal for a race and it was around his neck. He was drinking Kool-Aid. God's glory was all over him. I must have looked at the picture thousands of times in the last two years. I touched it briefly, then went to my office and picked up the book that stays on my desk, *Intercessory Prayer* by Dutch Sheets. I'm afraid that if I put it away, I won't be able to find it when I need it. So it stays out in plain sight. I picked it up and it opened automatically to the page I loved.

> "The Scriptures indicate that our prayers accumulate. There are bowls in heaven in which our prayers are stored. Not one bowl for all of them, but 'bowls.' We don't know how many, but I think it very likely that each of us has our own bowl in heaven. I don't know if it's literal or symbolic. It doesn't matter. The principle is still the same. God has something in which He stores our prayers for use at the proper time."

I'd grabbed my Bible to check the Scripture. This couldn't be true! Someone would have told me!

Revelation 5:8: "And when He had taken the book, the four living creatures and the twenty-four elders fell down before the Lamb, having each one a harp, and golden bowls full of incense, which are the prayers of the saints."

I drew a huge heart around the Scripture in my Bible and went back to the book. It cited another Scripture, and again I looked it up in my Bible:

Revelation 8:3–5: "And another angel came and stood at the altar, holding a golden censer; and much incense was given to him, that he might add it to the prayers of all the saints upon the golden altar which was before the throne. And the smoke of the incense, with the prayers of all the saints, went up before God out of the angel's hand. And the angel took the censer; and he filled it with the fire of the altar and threw it to the earth; and there followed peals of thunder and sounds and flashes of lightning and an earthquake."

Yes, it was in my Bible. Then back to *Intercessory Prayer*:

"According to these verses, either when He knows it is the right time to do something or when enough prayer has accumulated to get the job done, He releases power. He takes the bowl and mixes it with fire from the altar . . . In answer to our requests, He sends His angels to get our bowls of prayer to mix with the fire of the altar. *But there isn't enough in our bowls to meet the need!*"

I love to learn God's truth by making mental pictures. Without even trying hard, in my mind I saw the huge bowl that Jon used to eat his cereal out of. It was no ordinary bowl, mind you. He'd asked me to get him a "Jethro Clampett bowl" to eat from; he had loved *The Beverly Hillbillies* on television. I had bought the biggest mixing bowl I could find, yellow with a blue stripe, deep and wide. Everyone in our house knew it was Jon's bowl.

Now I saw the yellow-and-blue bowl up in Heaven, surrounded by golden bowls lined with rubies. God couldn't tip Jon's bowl until it was full. And when it was full—glory! God would tip it, and His answers would tumble out onto Jon—onto us.

So I'd started praying once again. No, I didn't feel like it; I was tired of praying and hanging on. Nevertheless, I prayed, using the new word I thought God had given me.

Months before, while praying one day it seemed God said to me, *Pray for My overshadowing on Jon.* Maybe it had been my imagination. I didn't know what it meant, so how could I pray it? I asked Gene what it meant. He didn't know. I called some minister friends of ours. They had no idea. I was stumped. I began to look through the index of all my books and Bibles. Nothing on *overshadow.* Surely it had just been my imagination. You couldn't pray for God to overshadow someone. He'd only overshadowed— that is, His Holy Spirit had overshadowed—the Virgin Mary.

One day I was rereading *Intercessory Prayer.* I decided to check for *overshadow* in the index.

"Overshadow, page one twenty-five!" How had I missed that? I broke out in gooseflesh and turned quickly to page 125 in the book.

"Overshadow is the Greek word *episkiazo* which means to cast a shade upon; to envelope in a haze of brilliancy; to invest with supernatural influence. . . . It is also used in Acts 5:15 when people were trying to get close to Peter—in his shadow—that they might be healed. Have you ever wondered how Peter's shadow could heal anyone? It didn't. What was actually happening was that the Holy Spirit was 'moving' out from Peter—hovering—and when individuals stepped into the cloud or overshadowing, they were healed."

Oh, my Father, overshadow Jon wherever he is now. Call his name. Hover over him with Your mighty Holy Spirit, set him free, restore him to what the two of You have known . . .

Another prayer went into the giant yellow-and-blue prayer bowl up in heaven.

Father, who would ever imagine that a "Jethro Clampett" bowl could have a spiritual meaning? I can see the mixing bowl up in heaven with Jon's name on it, so I know You're putting one more prayer into it. Sometimes I come so close to giving up on prayer—and Jon. Keep me praying . . . believing . . . hoping.

THE GENUINE | 37
BIRTHDAY PRESENT |

THE CALL FROM JON had brought back a memory of another call from him, years ago. "Collect call from Jon," the operator had said.

"Yes, of course I'll pay," I'd answered excitedly. Jon's calls from college had been infrequent and short. Usually he only phoned to tell me that he'd be home for the weekend. I always hoped that we'd have a real conversation on the phone someday. I was excited because I was certain Jon would be coming home this weekend: It was his and Jeremy's nineteenth birthday. "Mom, plan a real party," Jon had asked several weeks before. "Invite all the family and make reservations at some good restaurant, okay?" I'd made all the arrangements; I even ordered a cake to be presented at the restaurant. I was so excited that I imagined Jon and I wouldn't argue this weekend. Just maybe this weekend would be good for us. Surely Jon and I wouldn't fight about grades, his newfound freedom, or moral issues. I planned to take him shopping for a new bike. All the students at his college rode bikes. Besides, I knew he wanted one.

"Hi, Jon," I said with real enthusiasm, feeling very motherly.

"'Lo, Mom." A long silence told me instantly that everything wasn't okay. My excitement fizzled quickly. "Er . . . Mom . . . I'm not coming home for my birthday."

"But Jon, everything's planned . . ."

"Go ahead without me."

"But it's your birthday."

"I have other plans." His tone of voice told me not to proceed with the conversation. Immediately, I knew I wouldn't approve of the new plans.

Shifting rapidly to my angry-but-controlled voice, I said curtly, "Very well, Jon. Happy birthday. Good-bye."

Everyone was stunned that Jon wasn't at his party. "Jon sure missed a good steak dinner," one of my sons-in-law said as we left the Japanese steak house. "How come he didn't come?"

I shrugged and desperately tried not to be angry or hurt. I didn't succeed with either.

A few days after the boys' birthday, Jeremy asked, "Hey, Mom, what are you getting Jon for his birthday?"

"Nothing," I shot back.

"How can you do that, Mom?" Jeremy asked.

The following week Jon phoned again. I had decided that if he called, when the operator said, "Collect call from Jon," I'd say, "Jon who?"

My smug smile vanished as the operator said, "Collect call from Jon West. Will you pay?"

Why was Jon always one step ahead of me? "Yes, yes, of course," I answered.

"Hi, Mom," he said in a friendly, cheerful voice. He *was* coming home. "I got a ride home." There was a long pause. "Okay?"

"Okay, Jon." There was no warmth or excitement in my voice.

There was more silence. Then Jon blurted out, "Do you have a present for me, Mom?" He suddenly didn't sound nineteen anymore. Even though he'd told me loud and clear and often that most of my traditional values were obsolete, it seemed birthday presents were still "in."

"No." Silence again—two could play this game.

"Well,—see 'ya around four—okay?" he said in a hopeful voice, full of anticipation.

He's trying to con me. I will absolutely not get him a birthday gift.

Jon arrived at four the next day with a large basket full of dirty clothes and an even larger smile. After church on Sunday, when he realized that I hadn't done his laundry as usual, he silently began doing it himself. He put the colored and white clothes in together. I shuddered but pretended not to notice. I couldn't believe how he ironed his pants: He took them from the dryer and laid them on the carpet and sort of dragged his huge feet over them, almost as if he were skating in slow motion. I pretended that everyone ironed that way. Just as he finished his "ironing" his friend arrived to take him back to school. We hugged briefly, and he ran out to the car in the pouring rain. I didn't even tell him to wear a jacket.

After he was gone the house seemed very quiet. I sat stiffly on the edge of the sofa and looked at his bare footprints in the carpet. Finally I got up and placed my feet inside his prints. He wore size twelve now.

I wasn't at all prepared for the memory that surfaced clearly early Monday morning. The boys must have been about ten. Their daddy was picking out bikes for their birthdays. I recalled it vividly. Jerry and I were in the bike shop, and Jerry couldn't stop smiling. He selected a blue bike for Jon and a red one for Jeremy. I could see the slow smile that I loved—almost reverence—cross Jerry's face as he paid for the bikes. He ran his hand over them gently as though they were alive. I'd kept complaining about the price, but he was in another world—a world of bikes—and couldn't hear me.

Suddenly I was wide awake, sitting up in bed with the blue bike that Jerry had bought Jon years ago imprinted on my mind. Jerry had been dead almost four years, but thinking about that bike somehow brought me intense happiness. Then in my mind the bike changed into a large, ten-speed, lightweight one. I suddenly saw Jon riding the elegant bike *today*. I didn't seem to have control over my thoughts; how could Jon possibly receive a bike today? Unforgiveness left my heart and forgiveness and joy rushed in. I hopped out of bed and could hardly wait for the stores to open. Finally, at nine sharp, I phoned information in the town where Jon was in college. I asked the operator for the number of a bike shop, any bike shop. Then I dialed the number. The joy inside me was unmistakable.

A young man answered. I blurted out, "Hello. There's a blue bike there. Ten-speed, lightweight, large . . ."

"We have hundreds of bikes, ma'am."

"Well this one's for my son Jon. He's in college there. What kind of bikes do the boys there ride?"

"Tell me about your son," the patient young man said.

"He's six feet two inches tall, about two hundred pounds. Very strong"—I almost added "stubborn," but then didn't— "long legs, athletic, quiet . . . and he didn't come home for his birthday like he promised, and I've been angry all this time. I just forgave him early this morning, and he *has* to have a blue bike today."

"Hold on a moment, please." I waited in utter delight. I had forgotten how delicious forgiveness felt.

"Hello, ma'am. I believe I've found Jon's bicycle here."

"Wonderful! Could you put a big bow on it, and here's what I want you to write on a card. 'Happy Birthday, Jon. It's a late present, but it's a genuine birthday present. Your daddy would want you to have this one. Me too. I love you. Mom.'" The stranger read the message back to me.

"Oh, could you deliver the bike to the college today? Take it to the dean's office. I want someone who knows Jon to give it to him. The dean knows him and will know what to say. I'll call him and explain that you're bringing the bike."

"Yes, ma'am, I can deliver it today. I know the dean and right where his office is."

At six that afternoon the phone rang.

"Mrs. West?" I immediately recognized the dean's voice. We'd never met, but we had spoken on the phone many times about Jon. "I wanted you to know that one happy young man just rode a magnificent blue bike out of my office. Literally, Mrs. West. He rode it down the hall and right down the front steps."

"Oh, thank you for giving it to Jon for me! Is it okay? I don't know a thing about bikes."

"Okay? It's quite a bit more than okay. I know something about bikes."

I closed my eyes and imagined the scene that the dean described—"All Jon could say for a few minutes was 'For me? For *me?*' Finally, he confessed that he'd been thinking about having a bike all day. He looked at it for a long time silently and then touched it—well, actually he sort of stroked it. What a smile!"

At 6:45 the phone rang again. "Collect from . . ."

"I'll pay! I'll pay, operator," I fairly screamed at her.

"Hi, Mom. I got the bike! It's pretty neat. I rode it back to the dorm and then all around campus. I can't figure how you picked out such a good bike. You really aren't a bike person, ya know. Anyway—I really like it Mom. It's a great, *genuine* birthday present."

"Where's the bike now, Jon? Did you use the lock I sent? Is the bike locked up? Do you have the bike rack at your dorm?" I was back to my old self, asking too many questions.

"No, ma'am. I have it up in my room with me."

"Jon! You carried a bike up three flights of stairs? Isn't it too heavy? How could you . . ."

"Mom, Mom." His voice was gentle, calm. "It's really light. It doesn't weigh anything at all. Really."

"Oh." I smiled. Jon and I were at last having a real telephone conversation. Maybe the bike was as light as my heart with all the forgiveness surging around in it.

Father, thank You for happy memories of Jon and me, of the good times. Thank You for Jon's humor and for the actual easy conversation we had on the phone. We haven't had many like it. Would You give us another one please?

JERRY'S GARDEN | 38

JUST AFTER VALENTINE'S DAY 2004, Julie and Ricky moved into their new log house. They did a lot of the work themselves. Set in thick woods nearly half a mile from the road, it had the feeling of a retreat. Their daughters, Jamie and Katie, were away at school, but twelve-year-old Thomas was still at home.

One of my favorite things about the house was the writing loft Ricky had built for Julie overlooking the huge family room. There she set up her computer, her books, a comfortable recliner, and a couple of not-so-good paintings I'd done back in the seventies.

There was an extra-wide wraparound porch, and Julie seemed thrilled when I gave her the old square tables that had been my mother's. The paint was peeling, but she adored them. I also gave her the white straight-back chairs that Mother and I had used at the kitchen table on Myrtle Street, where we cut watermelons, where she helped me with my homework, and where I colored pictures while she cooked. I loved those chairs, and so did Julie. She put them in a corner of the front porch near an old table my mother had called the "wash table." It had held washing supplies and stood on an enclosed back porch. Mother didn't have a washing machine for most of her life. Then she got a pink one, and the little table stood next to it. I also loved the round beige enamel pan that held the wooden clothespins.

Julie had placed plants and flowers in an ancient container on the table. There were hanging ferns and red geraniums on the porch, a deacon's bench, and rusted antique farm implements.

But what Julie loved best was her little garden. She could hardly wait for Ricky to plow up the ground for her. Impatiently, she'd asked, "Can I plant seeds now? Put out tomato plants?"

"No, Julie," Ricky had said. "Not yet. Wait until I build up the soil." She'd waited, quietly but anxiously. Finally, they planted their garden, complete with a fence to keep out the deer.

"Guess what?" Julie said on the phone one morning. "Everything's coming up, all green and healthy! My tomato plants have tiny tomatoes on them. It's a real garden, Mother, just like Daddy would have planted. I wish he could see it.

"Sometimes I talk to him, just as though he's there. I say, 'Look, Daddy! Look at my garden. I must have inherited your green thumb. I wish I'd been more interested in your gardens through the years. You loved them and worked so hard and none of us really appreciated them like we should have. I wish I had memories of you and me in the garden. I'm going to pretend you can hear me and that you can even see my garden. Isn't it wonderful?'"

I was silent for a moment. Then I found a voice. "He'd be so proud of you, Julie. He'd stand out in the scorching sun and eat a tomato right out of the garden and let the juice run down his chin, smiling. . . ."

"I know, Mother. . . . Do you wish now that you'd been more . . . ?"

"Oh yes, of course, Julie. But I wished that while he was still alive. There's so much I would have done differently. After he was gone I did a lot of thinking about his garden and my . . . attitude."

I had hated Jerry's vegetable garden with a passion. When we moved to Lilburn back in the seventies, most everyone had a small garden out back. Jerry said that we should plant one too.

"No thanks," I'd declared. "I'm not a garden person." I'd hoped that would be the end of it. I should have known better!

Undaunted, he went out and bought seeds and an old, used tiller and began to till up a corner of our backyard. He was so optimistic, he even bought a small freezer to store the bounty. I threw a couple of loaves of store-bought bread into the shiny, new freezer—all I ever intended to contribute.

Smiling, Jerry talked about how great it would be to have homegrown vegetables year round. He'd grown up with a father who also gardened and a mother who adored filling the freezer. "Who's going to pick the stuff and put it in the freezer?' I asked, arms folded stubbornly.

"You might learn to enjoy it one day," he smiled.

I knew better.

Jerry spent countless hours in his garden. Once, when he had to work late every night at the office, he came home and tended his tomato and bean plants by moonlight, whistling "Blueberry Hill." I watched from an upstairs window, convinced he was wasting his time and energy. I did manage to remember when we'd danced to Fats Domino singing that song when I made the memorable trip to VPI for a dance weekend.

His garden was the talk of the neighborhood. The green bean stalks were so tall that I had to look straight up to see the tops. The tomatoes were deep red, perfectly round, and juicy. Everything grew well in Jerry's garden, but the butter beans were his all-time favorite. Home-grown butter beans and the University of Georgia Bulldogs football team were two of the most exciting things in his life. I hated football and the Georgia Bulldogs almost as much as I hated that garden.

The years rolled by, and Jerry went on picking butter beans without me. Often our children helped him shell them, and together they put package after package in the freezer with all the fanfare of people putting the Hope Diamond in a vault.

When Jerry became sick so suddenly, he'd assured me that it was nothing much. I couldn't shake the feeling that we were dealing with something big. Finally, after numerous CAT scans, the horrible mass had shown up in his brain.

I watched his every movement, willing him to live, pleading with God. Terrified. Asking God, *how will life ever make sense again?*

Jerry went on like always, laughing, whistling "Blueberry Hill," rooting wildly for the Bulldogs, playing with our collie, signing up the twins for Little League and, of course, tending his beloved garden. He'd never been a worrier. I don't think he even knew how to worry. Never mind; I could do it for both of us.

One day we came home from one of his hospital stays and plopped down on the sofa. "What do you want to do?" I'd asked, staring straight ahead, thinking: *This can't really be happening.* "I think the Bulldogs are playing. If you'd like, I'll watch the game with you."

I turned to glance at Jerry. He gave me his big, easy smile. "I'm going to pick butter beans," he said, as if this were just another early-autumn Saturday.

I looked at him. *Really* looked at him. He wasn't afraid. He never asked, "Why me?" He wasn't faking it. He wasn't even being brave for me. He was just very simply excited about his butter beans.

He stood, only a little unbalanced, grabbed onto the sofa to steady himself, then started toward the back door. "I'll go with you," I said, still terrified of what my future held without him.

"You don't like to pick butter beans, Mannie!" he'd exclaimed, turning to look at me. Then he burst out laughing, like he always did when he was really happy. He'd held out his hand and waited for me to catch up with him.

"I . . . I . . . changed my mind." I'd never wanted to do anything so much in my life as pick butter beans with my husband.

Out in his tall, green garden we went to work under the broiling Georgia sun. Creepy things crawled over my feet; I'm sure I saw at least one snake. I got so hot I saw spots, and my back, arms and legs ached. I sweated. Every time my gaze met Jerry's, he smiled enormously. Once he winked at me. Finally he announced that we were through, and we carried our reward inside.

Sitting at the kitchen table, Jerry and I began shelling the huge mound of butter beans. *I could do this every day for the rest of my life and be happy and content*, I suddenly realized as my eyes lingered on my husband's large, square, freckled hands easing the beans out of their shells.

I knew sitting at that old oak kitchen table that this was going to be a memory—a cherished one. It was going to be one of the high points, one of the loveliest times in our twenty-five-year marriage.

Jerry died the following July. We still had some of those butter beans in the freezer.

Father, I have a new appreciation for gardens. I wish I'd had it years ago. I guess You like them too; I can't imagine what Eden must have looked like.

39 | JON'S GARDEN

"Mom, I'm going to make you a flower garden while I'm here," Jon announced enthusiastically. "With a rock wall, new flowers—your garden needs work."

Indeed it did. I'd often imagined finding someone who'd really love to work in small gardens. Mine needed so much done: weeding, taking out dead plants, creating a new look. Someone who loved doing that kind of work was almost impossible to find. We could always find someone to do yard work when Gene got behind on it, but someone who liked the tedious labor of working in a small garden didn't seem to exist.

I had no idea Jon had a talent for gardening. It was unbearably hot that July. The humidity was terrific. Mostly I thought Jon was just talking but didn't intend to follow through.

The unbelievable was happening. Sitting in the tub the day before, I'd opened the window for our new cat, Girl Friend. She adored sitting in the window looking out while I'm bathing. One *meow* from her and I automatically opened the window and she hopped in it gratefully. I'd looked up at the blue sky through the tall trees in our backyard and prayed a spontaneous prayer: *Oh, Father, tomorrow's my birthday. It would be just too wonderful if Jon phoned and really wanted to go to Dunklin, if he really acknowledged that he was an addict and wanted to return to that city of refuge where You helped him so much two years ago.* I even imagined answering the phone—the whole conversation. Later that morning I wrote in my prayer journal the desire of my heart.

The day after my birthday Jon did call, collect from a pay phone. "Mom, I'm ready to go to Dunklin." He'd phoned three or four times in recent months, hinting that he might be ready to return for the nearly one-year program. But I never believed he was serious. Mostly he needed a place to live.

That day there seemed to be something different about his voice, though. I put Gene on the phone. He looked at me and nodded and gave a thumbs-up sign. Gene began writing down directions, and I heard him say, "Jon, it'll take us about two hours to get to you, but we will be there."

Oh, Lord! Did You hear? He's ready for help—desperate. Here we come, Jon. Thank You, God!

When we found the house Jon had described, I was shocked. It was a large house, almost a mansion. "He says the utilities have been cut off for some time. He has to vacate tomorrow. His roommate is long gone," Gene explained.

I nodded, looking out the window at Jon. He stood in the driveway, wearing a wide-brim straw hat and an even wider smile, a tee shirt, knee-length jeans, and sandals. Gene hopped out to help Jon put his few things in the back of our station wagon. Almost all his belongings were gone now. I noticed he appeared to have good use of the hand he'd almost lost to the flesh-eating bacteria.

I hopped in the backseat because Jon's legs were so long and I wanted him to feel the cool blast of the air conditioning; the noon heat was overwhelming. "I'll sit in the back, Mom," he said with a grin. I saw then that his hand was deeply scarred. Two fingers appeared not to move.

"It's okay," I said. "I'm already back here." From the backseat I studied the back of Jon's head. I longed to lean forward, kiss it, and hug him and tell him how much I admired him for never complaining. But something held me back. It wouldn't be good to become too emotional now. After some small talk, I made myself keep quiet. My eyes met Gene's in the rearview mirror, and he smiled and nodded slightly.

Just as we drove up the driveway of our house, Jon announced his intentions about the garden. "Maybe I can bathe the dog too. I want to work."

That afternoon Jon and Gene went to the garden center and bought stones for the garden and flowering plants—daisies, zinnias, gardenias, roses, little purple flowers, black-eyed Susans—and lots of mulch. Jon worked slowly, deliberately, painstakingly. I had no idea he knew how to garden. From time to time I brought him lemonade. He barely stopped working to gulp it down.

Every day he phoned Dunklin, asking to be readmitted. So many calls were coming in—twenty to forty a day—that it was hard to get the admissions people on the phone. Finally Jon spoke with someone he knew who said, "You keep calling back every day. We need to know you mean business, Jon."

Sure enough, he did—without complaining. The garden was coming along beautifully, and it appeared that Jon was too. He was respectful and helpful. He almost never stopped working. He made his bed nearly perfectly and washed his own clothes and folded them better than I could have. He laughed a lot, ate enormous amounts of food, and went to bed early.

After about two weeks the garden was nearly complete. Jon had draped sagging blue morning glories carefully over the picket fence. Everything he'd planted was blooming. When he saw me watering the plants late one afternoon, he said, kindly but firmly, "No, Mom. Not that hard." Then he adjusted the hose so that it sprayed softly, like rain. "Gently," he explained.

It was almost sundown. Jon, brown from working outside so much, looked content beneath his straw hat, like his father had when he'd finished working in his vegetable garden. "Hang on," I shouted. "Stay right there." I ran inside.

I grabbed a little blank wooden sign from the tool closet and quickly painted JON'S GARDEN—7/7/04 on it. Then I hurried back outside and hung the little sign on the picket fence, just over the birdbath and red-and-yellow zinnias.

Jon laughed. "You don't have to call it my garden, Mom."

"But it is, Jon. You revived it and made it beautiful. Actually, it feels like much more than a garden . . ."

"It is, Mom. It's a place to meet God—to return to Him and get things right."

I knew at that moment that I'd always be able to come to Jon's garden and find God—and Jon.

After supper, Jon said, "Oh, Mom, Gene, did I show you the Bible I found?" He went to get it and laid it in my lap. "I don't even know where I found it. It belonged to a strong believer, though; it's underlined."

Jon handed me the Bible, and I thumbed through it. There was a name inscribed in front, and many of the pages were marked and annotated. Then I looked in the very back. In an incredibly beautiful handwriting there was a Scripture indeed:

Though the fig tree should not blossom
And there be no fruit on the vines,
Though the yield of the olive should fail

And the fields produce no food,
Though the flock should be cut off from the fold
And there be no cattle in the stalls,
Yet I will exult in the Lord,
I will rejoice in the God of my salvation.
The Lord God is my strength,
And He has made my feet like hinds' feet,
And makes me walk on my high places.
                                    —HABAKKUK 3:17–19

Father, my joy is about to explode. I can hardly believe that Jon brought this Bible to show Gene and me, and there's the very Scripture I thought about basing a book on! How can this be? How can I doubt You when things seem dark? Oh, Father, I can go so very far with this encouragement. You are working in Jon's life. Mine too.

PART TEN

"AND MAKES ME WALK ON MY HIGH PLACES"

40 | A SKY-BLUE EIGHTEEN-WHEELER

JON'S GARDEN HAD ALMOST ERASED my memories of the things that happened before he came to stay with us.

One evening months before, the doorbell rang just as Gene and I were ready for bed. I heard Gene open the door and then Jon's booming, happy-sounding voice. We hadn't seen or heard from him in months; we didn't even know where he was. At one time I wouldn't have believed it was possible to live like that. I would have cried, screamed, begged, manipulated, done anything to try to help Jon.

Actually, I'd done all that years ago when Jon was out in the "twilight zone." I was sure that I—supermom—could get through to him. Nothing had helped.

Learning that I couldn't help Jon took years and years. I'd had twenty-two plans, good plans, crafty plans. None had worked. I had to decide if I wanted to go on with my life or fall apart. Sink or swim. "Get bitter or get better," as the lady with the white picket fence had put it.

I chose to swim; I chose to get better. But I told God I couldn't do it if He didn't come through for me.

He came through, but not until I was totally desperate to let go of Jon, not until I had no more plans.

Jon's beautiful voice filled our house and my heart. "Hi, Gene. How 'ya doing, buddy?"

Gracious, merciful Gene answered, "Jon! How are you? Come on in." I heard them in the kitchen; Gene warming up some homemade soup, making a sandwich, pouring soda, cutting chocolate cake. I remained frozen on the sofa, my feet tucked under me, grateful that Jon had food.

I heard Jon putting his dishes in the sink. Then they both came into the living room, and Jon sat down in the brown recliner, like old times. He was so much thinner, but his warm smile touched me like morning sunshine. Stretching and yawning, he said, "Think I'll spend the night, Mom."

God, give me Your strength. "You can't stay here, Jon."

"Mom. . . ."

I picked up the phone and said the unthinkable. "I'm going to call the police if you don't leave now," I desperately longed to add, "*son.*"

He got up, smiled, patted the cat, and said over his shoulder, "'Night, Mom, Gene."

I listened to him go out to the driveway and get into his borrowed car. He had trouble starting it. I knew he had nowhere to go. This was the life he had chosen. I could not—would not—help him continue to be an addict.

But now Jon was here, waiting to go to Dunklin. We were enjoying each other like normal people.

Then the call came; Jon could go to Dunklin for an interview. He was certain the interview was a formality. "I'm in," he told us. "They interview everyone. It's the rules. Man, that place has rules."

That Tuesday at 5:15 A.M. we left for Okeechobee, Florida. Ten hours later, we drove up to the familiar World War II era buildings of Dunklin Memorial Camp. We ate in the mess hall that night, at the table we'd eaten at when we'd visited Jon before. People came over to welcome Jon back.

Jon's interview was scheduled for early the next morning. Gene and I had been asked to sit in on it. I could hardly sleep in our small motel room on the Dunklin grounds. *In the morning*, I thought to myself, happily.

But the interview got off to a rough start and went down hill from there. Jon's answers, even his body language, were way off base. He looked too relaxed, almost indifferent, in his straight-back chair. He wouldn't look anyone in the eye. No, he didn't think he'd been rebellious. He objected to some of the Dunklin programs and rules. He didn't seem grateful for the chance to be readmitted.

Gene and I stared at each other in silent horror, not saying a word. "Man, what's going on?" one of the two staff members conducting the interview asked Jon. "You know the answers. You know what we expect, what we must have if we're going to admit you. You could teach most of these courses, Jon. You aren't giving us anything to work with."

I looked at the man asking the questions and saw the pain and disappointment in his brown eyes. "We can't accept you, Jon. Maybe another time, when you're really ready for help. When you're humble. When you're ready to be restored."

I didn't think I could move. But somehow I managed to get up out of the chair and walk out of that tiny office with Gene and Jon. *This can't be happening, God. It's a mistake. Jon will run back, humble himself, beg. That's all it would take.*

Back in our motel room I slung clothes into a suitcase while Gene loaded our station wagon. We'd been there not quite twenty-three hours. Jon walked into the room and said casually, "Mom, when we get back . . ."

I took a deep breath and said, "You can't go back with us. You're on your own, Jon."

He turned and walked out of the room, then came back. "Mom, I love you."

I ran to him, hugged him, began to cry and beg. "Please Jon, please, please . . ."

He stiffened, took my arms from his around his neck, and walked away.

Gene came in and said, "I'll take him to a bus station. That's it." The camp was twenty-five miles from civilization.

"No, I can't see him again! I've relinquished him so many times, and I have to do it again—now. I have to. There's no other way."

Quickly, Gene and I grabbed our luggage and got into the car. As we pulled away, Jon walked down the hot, sandy road to ask permission to use the office phone, the only one in camp. "What am I suppose to do?" he called out to us. His voice was calm. There's was even a little humor in it.

"Whatever," I managed, my voice cracking.

"Well, praise God," we heard him say. I rolled up the window, not daring to look back.

Gene and I drove silently mile after mile. Finally he asked, "Do you want me to go back, honey?"

"No. Just keep driving."

This isn't what I had in mind, Lord. Not leaving him practically on the side of the road. I know he only has ten dollars. God, You have to help me give him up again. You must be bigger than this anguish.

We'd been driving for a few hours when Gene said, "We need gas, Marion. I'm going to stop."

"No! Don't stop, please. Keep going. You can go a little farther."

So we rode on in silence, staring straight ahead. There was a lot of traffic on the road, and I noticed a sky-blue truck just ahead. *Where is he, Lord? If I just knew where he is, that would be enough.*

There in the middle of Highway 95, God gave me a rather strange idea. *Okay, Lord. When we reach the front of this eighteen-wheeler*—I squinted my eyes to read the words on the front door—*from Omaha, Nebraska, at that exact moment, I'm relinquishing Jon to You. Regardless of the circumstances, I'm going to trust You.*

As we passed the truck my cell phone rang. "Hi, Mom. A friend wired me money, and someone from Dunklin drove me to the bus station."

Oh, Lord, You are so totally faithful. Thank You. Thank You.

We arrived back at home at 10:30 P.M. In the morning the phone rang. "Mom, I'm in Macon. I had a five-hour wait in Jacksonville. I don't know what to do when I get to the bus station in Atlanta."

I longed to tell him that we'd come to Atlanta, that we'd bring him home again. But instead I answered coldly, "You had lots of answers at the interview." The words tasted nasty, bitter.

I began to feel like stone—cold, emotionless, tearless. I went into the room Jon had been using. He'd made the bed. I stripped off the sheets viciously, as though they were somehow the enemy. Then I fell on the bed as if I'd been knocked down by an invisible blow. I lay there, holding tightly onto the pillows. *Jon, Jon. Oh, Jon!* I squeezed the pillows, burying my face in them. Unexpectedly, my pent-up tears erupted—the noisy kind, with racking sobs.

Why couldn't an addict be all bad? All lying? All manipulative? All selfish? Why does he have to have deep rivers of sweetness?

When my tears were spent, I took the bed linens to the washing machine, dumped them in, and started it. It was still early morning.

I went outside to Jon's garden. I picked up the hose and turned on the water, letting it trickle slowly over the flowers the way Jon had showed me. I picked off a few dead flowers and noticed the buds ready to blossom. Eyes closed, I inhaled the aroma of the roses and gardenias. The sweet scent of the flowers calmed me from the inside out. I opened my eyes and read the little sign: JON'S GARDEN—7/7/04.

God was here for me, and so was Jon, the real Jon, whom I believed—I still believe—God would restore.

Father, we're starting all over again. The disappointment is so real I can taste it. But I must choose to trust You, not my feelings. Jon needs hinds' feet. So do I.

41 | ALL THESE MEMORIES

JEREMY CALLED early the next morning. "Mom," he whispered, "Jon showed up here at my apartment last night."

"How did he get there?"

Silence. Then, "He walked."

"From the bus station?" I asked with disbelief.

"Yes, all that way—fifteen or twenty miles. He was at my front door at nearly midnight. I knew he'd come here. I knew it."

"What did you do?"

"I couldn't refuse him. He was out of breath and looked really tired, about to drop. I let him in. I'm sorry. Are you mad?"

"No, Jeremy. I'm sorry for you. You don't need this. You're doing so well now."

"I know. It's stressful, but it would about kill me not to help him."

No need to give the tough love speech; Jeremy knew it all. "Thanks for calling, Jeremy. Hang in there. I love you."

"Who was it?" Gene asked.

"Jeremy."

"Jon's there?"

Neither of us said anything. It had all been said many times before. I was fresh out of words, ideas, speeches, solutions. . . .

"You okay?"

"I am. I'm going to swim. I choose to swim. Sinking won't solve anything."

"I'm sorry, honey."

I nodded, and he knew to just let me be quiet. Intrusive thoughts had been my downfall for years. I'd let one little negative or fearful thought in—for just a moment, I always thought—and once in my mind, the thought reproduced like kudzu. Already the thoughts of "what if" were buzzing around my mind like bees after honey. It would be so easy to let my guard down and let fear have its way.

But I hadn't come this far to give in now. I walked back to my home office and looked at pictures of my children when they were toddlers. My eyes lingered on Jeremy and Jon, their matching haircuts, outfits, skinned knees and smiling eyes. Their innocent little hands. . . . My thoughts flew back to their childhood. . . .

Once I'd been frying chicken for supper when I suddenly realized it was too quiet in the house. Jon and Jeremy were never quiet unless they were asleep or getting into trouble. I thought about the quiet as I floured another piece of chicken. The thought came to me: *Go love your boys.* I considered that for a few seconds. How often did I tell them that they were doing something good? How often did I stop to tell them that I loved them?

Again the overpowering thought: *Go love your boys.* I liked the thought, and decided that I'd do just that as soon as I put all the chicken in to cook. But the thought wouldn't go away: *Go love your boys now. Hurry. Right now! This instant.*

The thought was like a message on a tickertape machine. It wasn't just a passing thought; it was more like a command. It grew stronger and stronger. I didn't understand the urgency of the message. In the back of my mind I thought, *How silly to wash flour off my hands to go love my boys right now.* But I was doing it, and then I was running to find them.

I found them in the laundry room. Jon was standing by the dryer, counting backwards. He looked up at me in a strange way when I entered the tiny room. I sensed a fear I didn't understand. "Where's Jeremy?"

He didn't answer. Then I opened the dryer and saw Jeremy in his space helmet sitting with his knees drawn up under his chin. He was holding on to all the things he planned to take with him into space. He looked surprised to see me, but gave me a big smile.

I remained bent over for a few seconds staring at him and praying. *Thank You, Lord; oh, thank You.* I had wondered why Jon had been counting as I entered the room. He was about to blast Jeremy off into space. He could easily reach the dryer's "on" button.

Deep relief and gratitude flooded through me, then anger; but the command had been, *Go love your boys.* So I sat on the floor holding both of them and talking with them about what might have happened. And I told them how much I loved them.

As I looked through the pictures, another memory came to my rescue. Just as we'd begun our meal in a restaurant, Jon spilled his milk. It was Sunday, and he was wearing his best clothes. The milk ran off the table onto his lap. His eyes met mine and he sat frozen in the chair. He made no attempt to move out of the way of the dripping milk. Jon was the champion milk-spiller in our family—he always got so excited about eating. Spilled milk or spilled anything always hit an ugly nerve in me.

Instantly hands reached out to help Jon. A waitress ran quickly with napkins; his daddy lifted him from the chair; Jennifer grabbed his coat from the back of the chair.

I neither moved nor spoke. From underneath his daddy's arms, as Jerry lifted him, Jon's big brown eyes looked at me—waiting.

Lord, help me. Please.

When I managed to flash Jon a smile, it surprised even me. And it felt wonderful. His little face melted into a relieved smile, an apologetic smile, a proud smile and finally a thank-you-Mama smile.

From the corner of my eye I noticed someone watching the incident. I glanced in that direction. A mother and father eating with their children looked at us. The mom smiled quickly at me. Her smile conveyed, *Congratulations! I know it wasn't easy. Good going.*

I shot her a smile back and looked away. I wondered if she ever prayed about things like spilled milk. Then I noticed that she and her family bowed their heads and prayed over their meal. I felt certain she prayed over spilled milk too.

We continued eating our meal without a cross word or look. Jon didn't complain about his wet clothes. He sat erect and proud. He ate carefully, and every time I looked his way, we exchanged smiles all over again.

Another picture brought a different memory into my heart: the Sunday after I'd learned that Julie and Ricky planned to be married right after she finished high school.

Ricky Garmon was a year older than Julie. We loved him; we'd just assumed that Julie would attend college before they married. After all, she was going to be her high school's valedictorian. Suddenly she was wearing a diamond ring. I'd done well for the last few days. But I hurt deep down in a manner I'd never experienced before.

That afternoon I fought the anguish in my heart and tried to swallow the sobs that rose in my throat. Tears began to spill down my face and onto my dress. My family moved about, close by. I wiped the tears away quickly. *I will not cry and mess up my face. It's almost time for church. No time for a scene.* I shut my eyes tightly to keep in the tears. In the blackness of my mind there stood Julie in a diaper. She fell, but got up and tried standing all over again.

I saw her again as a little girl jumping rope. "Down in the meadow where the green grass grows . . ." Her red hair bounced in the sun. Then I saw her in a pink nightgown, tucked in bed with a Pooh Bear. In my mind she ran in from school and told me she'd been elected to the bus patrol. A big white belt hung from her small waist. I heard her practicing the piano and then calling to me from out in the yard, where she was practicing a new cheer in her blue and white uniform.

Then I thought: *I won't be able to go into her room much longer and call her to get up or watch her peering into her makeup mirror. There won't be any of her clothes lying around.* Since she became engaged, I hadn't mentioned that she should pick up her clothes. I'd just pick up a blouse or a pair of jeans almost gently and then sit on the edge of her unmade bed holding them. No lectures about neatness formed inside me. Sitting on her bed, alone in her room, I'd looked around at every detail. Even the mess seemed sweet.

As I perched on my kitchen stool, my mind screamed, *I won't listen for her to come in at night. She won't ask me to plug in her curlers anymore. She won't come into the kitchen and talk to me and ask, "What's for supper?" She won't hurry in from school, put her books on the kitchen table, beaming, and ask, "Guess what, Mom?"*

Now I couldn't hold back the pain. Tears gushed uncontrollably, and I made terrible noises with my throat. I'd never cried in front of my family before.

Somebody has to put an arm around me and tell me everything is okay. Somebody has to! Please, dear Lord.

Jennifer ran quickly upstairs. Nine-year-old Jeremy came into the kitchen, then moved quietly into the den and sat watching me. I heard my husband go to some other part of the house. I opened my eyes again for a moment and saw that Julie had joined Jeremy. She sat perfectly still, erect, staring straight ahead as though she were taking an eye exam. The cat crept quietly out of the kitchen.

I wanted to disappear, to hide in the pantry, but I seemed to be glued to the kitchen stool, and the terrible noises just kept coming from me.

I felt an arm touch my shoulder and a warm, firm hand rested on my cold, clenched one. A sturdy body stood close to me, not wavering an inch. A rhythmic pat began on my back. Then I put my face onto the shoulder of my other son—Jon.

Jon. My son who talked too loudly and fast, who spilled his milk—who wore out a pair of shoes in four weeks. . . .

He spoke confidently and softly. "It's going to be okay, Mama. It really is. You'll see. And you don't have to cry no more now." Gallantly, ever so gently, he spoke the words, while patting my back without missing a beat.

No more tears or sobs came from me. I became still, quiet. A tiny spark of joy ignited in my heart. I looked into Jon's face, inches from mine. There was ketchup on his mouth. I smiled at him. "I know, Jon. I'm going to be okay, but I needed someone to tell me . . . and to understand. Thank you."

Jon nodded, and with one final pat on my back, he walked out of the kitchen. Both his shoelaces flopped behind him. I never could fully explain to anyone, even to myself, what happened. I just know that Jon's simple words became alive in my heart. I experienced a healing late that Sunday afternoon sitting on my kitchen stool—and we hadn't even gone to church.

Father, memories are like a good medicine that works quickly. I don't want to deal with life right now. So I'm grateful that I can go back and walk through sweetness with Jon. Oh, if he were just ten again! I'd play ball with him and listen to him and smile at him and cook him anything he wanted. I'd never frown or shout. I'd hug him whether or not he hugged me back. Can You tell him that I love him?

BEYOND THE | 42
BLACKBERRY PATCH |

As a child I often observed women confidently mothering their broods, knowing exactly what to buy in the grocery store, or driving with complete assurance to a destination with a car full of squealing children.

I told myself, "Someday I'll be doing that too. I'll be all grown up, married, and have children." But in my mind's eye, I wondered: How can that ever be?

For it seemed I would always be a skinny, shy little girl merely peeking into the awesome world of adulthood.

I used to reason, *I can't just stay a child—no one ever does. Growing up must happen sometime. But I can't imagine being one of them—an adult. I can't believe I'll do grown-up things like drinking coffee or sitting around and being still for hours or wanting to take a nap. And I can't believe I'll ever put cold cream on my face. I don't know how to be a mother—and who will ever love me and want me for his wife?*

I tried not to think about the future too much, because deep down it frightened me terribly. I didn't like changes. I wanted to hold onto my childhood. I knew I would be content for the rest of my life to continue picking blackberries with the hot sun beating down on my back in the summer and marveling over seeing my own breath before me in the winter.

Zooming down a hill on skates, playing "kick-the-can" till

the stars came out, sleeping late, reading all day if I wanted to, going to camp, feeding stray animals, rescuing drowning bugs, carefully cutting out a new book of paper dolls, and smiling to myself in a dark theater over Gene Autry's goodness was the only life I knew or understood.

I couldn't possibly see how I would give all this up in exchange for methodical grocery shopping, talking politely to other grown ladies, having permanents, and struggling with a child who had temper tantrums in the dime store.

As a teenager I occasionally thought about the future, about getting married and having children. But I decided that the future must be a long way off, because inside I still felt like a child.

When I went away to college, if I had to choose sides, I would have quickly said I belonged with the children of the world rather than the adults.

In my early twenties I loved someone who loved me, and we began to talk about marriage. The future I had imagined for so long was near—and yet it didn't seem too different from yesterday.

One evening years ago, I sat on my front steps and watched the sun disappear. The delicious coolness of the twilight touched me as the heat of the day faded away. Supper was over, the kitchen clean. I had even done some extra housecleaning and felt especially good about it.

I watched my husband move the sprinkler. We had just reseeded the front lawn. (Funny, as a child, I had taken grass for granted.)

Our thirteen-year-old daughter Jennifer sprinted across the street to her best friend's house. She leaned impatiently against the door and waited for it to be opened, confident that she would be welcomed inside.

Our eight-year-old twin sons, engaged in a ballgame across the street, would complain loudly when I called them in for a bath. (Maybe tonight I would say yes when they begged for ten more minutes.)

Our sixteen-year-old daughter Julie smiled slightly and waved good-bye to me from her boyfriend's car as they headed for the skating rink. (Could skating at a sophisticated rink, to the latest music, possibly be more fun that gliding on your skates down a sidewalk full of cracks that you could jump over?)

My cat rubbed contentedly against my knee. Looking down I noticed some new touch-me-nots had come up by the steps, so many more than last year. A neighbor waved from across the street, and I waved back enthusiastically.

For a few moments I saw my world and family as though they were a uniquely woven tapestry that I hadn't realized was of such dear workmanship—or so nearly complete. I marveled at each child and at my husband, bent over the sprinkler.

Contentment surged through me.

Suddenly, I became aware of the presence of God, and He seemed to say to me: *Remember when you couldn't understand how all of this would happen? When you were even afraid of it and wanted to turn back? Remember when this very moment was in a faraway future and you were a little girl sitting up in a tree, afraid— wondering how it would ever really happen?*

"Yes, yes, Lord," I almost shouted. "I remember." (He knew about that day in the Chinaberry tree!) Now my childhood seemed as incredible and as far away as the adult world once did.

Somehow, I'd entered this impossible world of grown-ups. And now I'm really here and yet I'm not aware of ever having let go of my childhood. My devotion to Gene Autry and paper dolls hasn't faded. I still like to skate and feed stray animals. I love to pick blackberries—and now I can whip up a cobbler with them. Being a child isn't very different from becoming an adult.

And then I became aware of a startling thought, so powerful that my heart beat rapidly and tears stung my eyes. *Someday, you'll leave this world and enter into My everlasting Kingdom. There's no need to be anxious now or try to figure it out. You can't. But it will happen just as surely and gently as you've moved from that world of childhood into the world of adults. My child, you can't imagine how wondrous it's going to be!*

Polly, my neighbor across the street, rang the doorbell. "I remembered how much you like figs and brought you some," she said.

I thanked her and invited her in, but she had to go. So I took the freshly picked figs into the kitchen and called Gene. "How appropriate," he said, smiling. "Sort of like a grand finale, isn't it?"

I nodded and then began to think, *What have I missed? What is God saying to me with this impromptu gift of figs?* I retrieved some notes at my desk and read them to Gene.

"Listen to this," I said excitedly. "'But figs do have flowers. Hundreds of hidden flowers line the hollow center of a green fig. . . When you bite into a dried fig, all the tiny seeds you find were once flowers.'"

How had I missed this before? Gene and I stared at each other, hunched over the figs. "Read it again," he said. I did.

He picked up one of the figs and bit into it. We both peered at the remaining half of the fig, our noses almost touching. There inside the fig were the blooms—tiny scrunched-up blossoms!

"The flowers are on the inside of the fig," I whispered, scarcely believing what I saw. Gene got a paring knife and cut through more of the figs. All of them contained the precious, tiny blossoms.

"Do you know what this means?" Gene asked quietly.

"Yes! Yes! It means that even though I can't see God doing a thing in Jon's life, or Jeremy's, He's at work. Behind the scenes, He's accomplishing incredible things, answering our prayers. I know He is!"

Gene nodded. I was jumping up and down, my heart pounding. I smiled, nearly giddy with my new knowledge. A few sentences slipped into my thoughts. They didn't seem to come from me.

I still whisper to those who will hear: I long to help you, child, to answer your prayers. Whatever you see or don't see, hang on to hope— to Me. Pray, child! Pray!

ACKNOWLEDGMENTS |

A HOST OF FRIENDS believed this book would be written years before it was begun. Others encouraged me once the task was undertaken. I think my faith resembled Sarah's when God told her she was going to have a baby: She laughed first, then exclaimed, "It's impossible!"

In the Introduction, I've written about the role Karen Barber played in making *Praying for My Life* a reality. There are some others whom I'd also like to thank:

My dear husband, Gene Acuff, also believed in this book. Once I started it and holed up in my office, he took phone calls, fed the dog and cat, kept the house in order and quietly brought me sandwiches, iced Pepsis and Milk Duds. He'd set the food down without speaking and leave quietly, sometimes blowing me a kiss. He endured my shutting him out of my life some days while I grumbled, "I can't do this."

How can I express my deep love and gratitude to my children, Julie, Jennifer, Jeremy, and Jon? Bless each one of you. I so admire and cherish each of you for special, yet different, reasons. Without you and our struggle there could be no *Praying for My Life*.

Amazing Andrew Attaway! He painstakingly edited my messy manuscript, correcting misspelled words and dangling participles, inserting commas and removing them. Thank you, Andrew, for taking my manuscript seriously. Never mind that it was typed on my beloved twenty-four-year-old IBM Selectric II, with uneven or no margins and Milk Duds smeared across some of the pages. I'm sure there was even cat fur wedged into it; my cat, Girl Friend, slept on the manuscript as I typed it. What I mailed Andrew should have been only a very rough draft—never meant for the eyes of an editor.

Friends at church, especially my small Sunday school class of women—Beverly Varnado, Claudia Woodruff, Jan Goggans, and Frieda Thornton, among others—prayed consistently for the book. They are some of the most stubborn women I've ever known and loved.

I'm forever grateful to friends whom I rarely see, but who wrote or phoned with powerful words of encouragement: Melba Fletcher, Marilyn Strube, Roberta Messner, Marci Alborghetti, "Dutch" and Linda Slade, and Sara Snipes.

Thank you, Marilyn Moore and Stephanie Samoy, for allowing me to get away with not using a computer.

Bless you, Tib Sherrill, for your genuine words of affirmation about this book when we met briefly in October 2004. I saw such steadfast faith in your eyes that I thought, *Maybe this will turn out okay after all.*

Thank you to my old pal Jim McDermott, now retired from Guideposts. I had the privilege of working with Jim for more than thirty years. His critiques of my articles kept me writing. I learned from his rejections, which were consistently gentle and constructive. And his acceptances were always filled with astonishing joy and anticipation.

And my gratitude and profound admiration go to Mickey and Laura Mae Evans and all the brothers at Dunklin Memorial Camp in Okeechobee, Florida, for whom prayer is life and restoration.

—Marion Bond West